Making
Teacher
Evaluation
Work

Making Teacher Evaluation Work

A GUIDE FOR Literacy Teachers and Leaders

Rachael Gabriel and Sarah Woulfin

HEINEMANN
Portsmouth, NH

Heinemann
361 Hanover Street
Portsmouth, NH 03801–3912
www.heinemann.com

Offices and agents throughout the world

The authors and publisher wish to thank those who have generously given permission to reprint borrowed material:

Figure 4.2: Six Evidence-Based Practices for Writing Instruction from "A Path to Better Writing: Evidence-Based Practices in the Classroom" by Steve Graham and Karen R. Harris in *The Reading Teacher*, Vol. 69, No. 4, pp. 359–365 (January/February 2016). Published by John Wiley & Sons, Inc. Reprinted by permission of the publisher.

Acknowledgments for borrowed material continue on p. xxii.

Cataloging-in-Publication Data is on file at the Library of Congress.
ISBN: 978-0-325-08879-2

Editor: Margaret LaRaia
Production: Vicki Kasabian
Cover design: Suzanne Heiser
Cover image: © Shutterstock/John T. Takai
Interior design: Shawn Girsberger
Typesetter: Shawn Girsberger
Manufacturing: Steve Bernier

Printed in the United States of America on acid-free paper

21 20 19 18 17 ML 1 2 3 4 5

While writing this book,
we frequently reflected upon our former students,
co-teachers, leaders, and mentors who we engaged with in schools.
This book is dedicated to the children and youth
who read in classrooms, libraries, playgrounds,
blanket forts, and subways
as steps toward attaining their goals.
And to the teachers and leaders
who create spaces, time, and supports
for each of these students to thrive today and in the future.

CONTENTS

Foreword by P. David Pearson   xi

Acknowledgments   xiv

INTRODUCTION   **Understanding Teacher Evaluation Policy**   xv

Logics of Evaluation   xv

Do We Measure and Sort or Support and Develop?   xvi

Why We Wrote This Book   xix

How to Use This Book   xx

Key Points   xxi

- How we got to where we are with teacher evaluation policies
- What these policies mean for teachers' literacy instruction

CHAPTER 1   **Teacher Evaluation Systems: From Policy to Practice**   1

Making Sense of Policy   2

Policy Knowledge for Teacher Evaluation   5

New-Generation Teacher Evaluation Policies   8

The Mechanisms of Teacher Evaluation   10

A Measure and Sort Approach to Learning About Policy   11

A Support and Develop Approach to Learning About Policy   12

Key Points   13

- What teachers and leaders need to know about policy
- How educators can learn about policies to advocate for themselves and their students

CHAPTER 2   **Implementing Teacher Evaluation Systems in Complex Contexts**   14

Distractions   14

Tools for Teacher Evaluation   15

Rubrics   *16*

Observation debrief conversations   *18*

Goals and Student Learning Objectives   19

Accountability in Balance   19

A Measure and Sort Approach to Implementing Teacher Evaluation Systems   20

A Support and Develop Approach to Implementing Teacher Evaluation Systems   21

Key Points   24

- Why time spent on teacher evaluation doesn't add up to positive changes in teaching and learning
- Priorities within the time-consuming process of teacher evaluation

- What leaders do to set teachers up for success in their classrooms
- What teachers and leaders do to promote the best conditions for literacy learning

CHAPTER 3   Environments for Effective Literacy Instruction   25

Setting Up an Environment for Literacy Learning   25

Access to a wide range of text types on a wide range of levels   26

Values that create literacy-focused environments   31

Time and space to build literate environments   35

A Measure and Sort Approach to Creating Environments for Literacy Learning   39

A Support and Develop Approach to Creating Environments for Literacy Learning   40

Key Points   41

- The active ingredients that make literacy instruction effective
- What each active ingredient looks like in a classroom observation

CHAPTER 4   Effective Literacy Instruction   43

How Teachers Use Time   44

Active Ingredients   45

Reading accurately with a purpose   45

Writing with a purpose and audience   51

Talking about text with teachers and peers   55

Discussing models of fluent reading and expert writing   56

Interventions that support individuals and focus on meaning   58

A Measure and Sort Approach to Ensuring Effective Literacy Instruction   62

A Support and Develop Approach to Ensuring Effective Literacy Instruction   63

Key Points   64

- How tools for evaluation set and limit what counts as effective instruction
- Questions that should be asked about the critical aspects of instruction that cannot be seen

CHAPTER 5   Observations of Literacy Instruction   66

Imperfect Tools for Classroom Observation   68

Understanding connections between instruction and achievement   68

Is quality really in the eye of the beholder?   73

Not whether, but how questions for teacher evaluation   74

A Measure and Sort Approach to Observing Classroom Instruction   76

A Support and Develop Approach to Observing Classroom Instruction   77

Key Points   79

- How leaders formulate feedback that teachers will hear and incorporate
- How teachers make something out of unwanted, inaccurate, or otherwise ineffective feedback

CHAPTER 6   Giving and Getting Effective Feedback   80

Giving Feedback   82

Feedback as learning fuel   82

Four actions for effective feedback   84

Getting Feedback: Fueling Learning in the Absence of Useful Feedback   90

A Measure and Sort Approach to Giving and Getting Feedback   91

A Support and Develop Approach to Giving and Getting Feedback   92

Key Points   93

CHAPTER 7 Setting Effective Goals for Literacy Learning 94

Literacy-Specific Challenges for Setting Effective Goals   95
  Most reliable measures of reading and writing artificially constrain tasks.   95
  Literacy development is unevenly distributed over time.   98
  Literacy development is distributed across in- and out-of-school experiences.   100
  Reading and writing aren't skills, they are coordinated accomplishments.   101
How to Set and Evaluate Effective Goals for Literacy Learning   103
  Goals focus and narrow efforts.   103
  Goals communicate priorities.   104
Varying Goals Over Time to Maximize Effectiveness   105
A Measure and Sort Approach to Setting Effective Goals   106
A Support and Develop Approach to Setting Effective Goals   107
Key Points   108

- Why goal setting is particularly difficult for literacy instruction
- How educators set goals that inspire, rather than restrict, ambitious teaching

CHAPTER 8 Evolving Policies to Improve Teaching 109

Assumptions and Realities of Teacher Evaluation Policies   110
Making Teacher Evaluation Work for You   112
Shifting the Focus of Evaluation   113
Looking Ahead to the Future   114

- How the teaching profession can strengthen itself within and outside of accountability policies

APPENDIXES 116

1A   Resources to Support Policy Knowledge   116

1B   Process for Becoming Informed About Policy   117

1C   Influences on Classroom Practice Discussion Starter   119

2A   Initiative Alignment Tool   120

2B   Evaluation Tool Cost and Benefit Discussion Starter   121

3A   Things to Look For/Questions for Discussion About Environments and Resources for Literacy in Your School   122

3B   Questions for Discussion About Classroom and School Libraries   123

3C   Cycles of Reading Success/Failure   124

3D   Allocated Versus Actual Timekeeper   125

3E   Criteria for Quality Sources of Online Texts   126

3F   Sources of Leveled Texts Online   127

3G   Coaches as Partners in Evaluation   128

4A Pocket Version of the "Look-Fors" for Key Ingredients of Effective Literacy Instruction   131

4B Accountability First and Just Read Case Study   133

4C Create Your Own Case Study   135

5A Surface Features and Underlying Processes   137

6A Structures for Framing Feedback as Learning Fuel   139

6B Questions to Ask When You Receive Poor Feedback   140

7A Goal Envisioning Worksheet   141

8A Rubric for Identifying High-Quality Professional Development   142

References   144

FOREWORD

Rachael Gabriel and Sarah Woulfin (two of my favorite young scholars who know and care as much about policy as they do about pedagogy) have collaborated to bring us a unique and remarkable book. Two attributes of the authors account for its uniqueness; their work is as well-grounded in theories of policy making as it is in the realities of classroom practice in today's schools. Not content to confine themselves to the ivory tower of the academy, they live and work in both worlds. This productive tension renders the book both thoughtful and useful. I could not offer higher praise for any book that aims to improve teaching and learning in our schools.

Titled *Making Teacher Evaluation Work*, it is a book about teacher evaluation designed to speak primarily to two audiences: (a) those charged with the responsibility of conducting teacher evaluation (principals, other supervisors, and coaches), and (b) teachers who will be the subjects (or recipients, depending on your approach) of evaluation systems. In a less direct way, it also speaks to those who operate preservice teacher education programs, for they will have to prepare novice teachers for the realities of evaluation in today's world of accountability.

The Journey

Across eight crisply written chapters, Gabriel and Woulfin take us on a journey that prepares us for the inevitability of teacher evaluation in our current world of accountability. That journey begins in the new world of teacher evaluation policy (what we seem to be doing and why), then reminds us that evaluation is situated in very complex contexts (these things called schools), and presents us optional frameworks for enacting our evaluation—all that in the first two chapters. The next three chapters (3, 4, and 5) constitute an excursion into the world of literacy—supportive environments, curriculum and pedagogy, and tools to use to observe and interpret literacy teaching and learning. Then the journey returns to effective evaluation practices in Chapters 6 and 7; here we learn the nuts and bolts of the feedback cycle (both giving and receiving), collaborative goal setting, and live, real-time observation. The book ends where it began—in the world of teacher evaluation policy—this time with a more positive and future-oriented spin. Even the most skeptical of teachers (been there, done that) leave the final chapter believing that teacher evaluation might even have a silver lining, allowing us as teachers to continually outgrow ourselves as professionals.

The Ethos

Gabriel and Woulfin offer us both text and subtext to educate us and to persuade us of the virtues of teacher evaluation. The text is the exposition of what constitutes good literacy practice (so evaluators will know *what* to look for) and good evaluation practice (so evaluators will know *how* to look at the *what*). The subtext is hidden in one of the major motifs in the book— the recurring juxtaposition of two contrasting models of teacher evaluation: *measure and sort* versus *support and develop*. They are careful to say that both models have merit, affordances if you will, and both have blind spots, constraints on their application. At the end of each chapter, they revisit this motif, telling us what it would mean, for example, to give feedback, set goals, conceptualize pedagogy, or observe teaching within a *measure and sort* versus a *support and develop* motif. It is a very useful motif, providing readers with a consistent and recurring tool for reflecting on the key ideas and practices in each chapter. However, as balanced as they try to be in unpacking the two models, one leaves the book with a pretty clear sense that *support and develop* is more desirable than *measure and sort. Or* perhaps that if *measure* (maybe not *sort*) is on the pathway to *support and develop*, then it can be tolerated, perhaps even exploited for the improvement of teaching.

The second implicit (but pervasive) tenet of the book's ethos is derivable from the first. Evaluation is more just and more useful when it is collaborative rather than hierarchical. In other words, evaluation should not be something that a supervisor does *to* a teacher; instead it should be what a supervisor does *with* a teacher—and for the purpose of improving teaching on the way to improving learning. Collaborative, not hierarchal, practices are much more consistent with the *support and development* principle than with the *measure and sort* principle. Two analogies seem relevant here— Tony Bryk and colleagues' (2015) construct of improvement science and the practice of formative assessment, as it has evolved through the work of Dylan Wiliam (2009) and Margaret Heritage (2010). In Bryk's approach to improvement science, all of the tools of reform—standards, assessments, and professional development—are focused on getting better at what we do through collaborative learning communities. The *support and develop* approach to teacher evaluation is likewise focused on continuous improvement. In a similar way, the formative assessment cycle of selecting learning goals, developing criteria for success, eliciting evidence, interpreting evidence, adapting and responding to needs—and then starting all over again has a similar patina of continuous improvement. Again, like the *support and develop* approach, the focus in formative assessment is on improving teaching and learning. These commonalities across these three different reform-oriented enterprises is a virtue, for it means that school communities can appropriate tools from other domains, like improvement science and formative assessment, to enhance their teacher evaluation agenda.

In short, on the face of it, considering just the text, this is a book about how to evaluate teachers justly and fairly. It provides us with a set of goals—what good literacy practices look like—and a set of tools—the nuts and bolts of good evaluation practices. But when we consider the subtext, the implications of the *support and develop* approach to teacher evaluation, the book serves as an invitation to outgrow ourselves as professionals, on the way to improving teaching on the way to improving learning. And that is why every serious classroom teacher and every serious literacy coach, school principal, and supervisor should read this book. Even better, the teachers, coaches, principals, and supervisors should read it together.

P. David Pearson

ACKNOWLEDGMENTS

An all-star team of teachers and leaders that we trust and admire gathered to give feedback on an early draft of this text; their words and margin notes stuck with us through the entire process. Thank you to Michael Berry, Lauren Francese, Stephanie McNamar, Katy Parkin, Lillie Stuart, and Kevin Thompson. This book would not be what it is without your generous investment of time, thought, and guidance. We were honored to write it to you, for you, and with you.

The MVP award goes, as ever, to Hannah Dostal, who listened to the entire book read aloud, offered feedback, challenged our thinking, edited multiple drafts, and knew what we were talking about even when we didn't. Thank you for believing in us and in this work from the beginning.

INTRODUCTION

Understanding Teacher Evaluation Policy

> ▶ *How did we get to where we are with teacher evaluation policies?*
>
> ▶ *What do these policies mean for teachers' literacy instruction?*

Logics of Evaluation

When Connecticut passed its new teacher evaluation law in 2011, we sat around a conference table with four other university professors—all policy analysts and former teachers in their own right—trying to sketch out a model that would capture the underlying logic of each part of the new policy. It took us two weeks, three meetings, ten Post-it posters, and about eighty emails back and forth to come up with several sketches of possible models, none of which were fully complete or fully compatible. Our attempts to clarify and graphically display the internal logic of the new teacher evaluation policy largely failed. In fact, Rachael's final draft was named the "illogic model," because it still contained question marks and arrows to nowhere from some of the policy's key components.

The illogic model highlighted crossed purposes and processes in the policy, but it also highlighted some glaring points of tension within the model. For example, the same measures of effectiveness are applied to teachers of all grades and all subjects. This creates strange absurdities like art teachers being evaluated in part on students' math scores and kindergarten teachers being evaluated using the same criteria as high school teachers. But it also creates significant difficulty when it comes to using teacher evaluation systems to support and develop individual teachers. For example, the structure, pace, and content of first- and tenth-grade science are not the same, yet they are evaluated using the same tools, which are likely to draw an evaluator's focus to the same indicators and sets of suggestions. Teaching all grades and content areas is not a singular, generic activity, so criteria for rating quality cannot be generic.

As we began the process of interviewing several hundred teachers and administrators across the state as part of an evaluation of the teacher evaluation pilot (Donaldson et al. 2013), we quickly began to see that the problem was not a lack of logic within teacher evaluation policies, but competing logics that explain the deeper values and aims of evaluation. We learned from educators in Connecticut that mixed messages about the purposes and processes of teacher evaluation have made teachers and leaders frustrated, confused, anxious, and often disillusioned about the entire process of evaluation.

Do We Measure and Sort or Support and Develop?

New-generation teacher evaluation systems invariably contain at least two competing logics: the logic of accountability and the logic of development. The logic of accountability holds that a state must set clear criteria for educator excellence, measure each educator against this criteria every year, and use this information to inform employment decisions like hiring, firing, promotion, and tenure. We call this the *measure and sort* logic for short, because it includes efforts to measure and sort teachers based on quality.

The logic of development holds that states and districts must offer support and learning opportunities for all educators to ensure positive student outcomes. We call this the *support and develop* logic for short, because it includes efforts to highlight existing expertise by offering recognition and addresses weak instruction by offering learning opportunities (e.g., mentoring, coaching, professional development activities; see Figure I.1).

	Measure and Sort	Support and Develop
Purpose of evaluation	• Use observations to assess quality of teaching • Assign a rating label to teachers based on the quality of their teaching	• Use observations to gain data on what to support teachers on • Connect to school improvement plan
Role of evaluator	• Observe instruction and assign a rating	• Observe instruction and conduct feedback conversation with teachers
Role of teacher	• Teacher as employee	• Teacher as professional learner

FIGURE **I.1** Measure and Sort Versus Support and Develop

The challenge of new-generation teacher evaluation systems is that both logics are obviously implied, and both could potentially lead to better outcomes, but when they are applied to the same set of tools, they cause conflict and thwart each approach's intended purposes. For example, consider the following situation a teacher shared with us at a workshop on preparing for classroom observations sponsored by a regional reading association (identifying details have been changed).

Allison, a fourth-grade teacher, was preparing for a scheduled classroom observation. To show off her best instruction, she arranged for the observation to occur in the second part of her lesson when students would be engaged in independent practice while she conferred with individuals one by one. She considers conferencing the most powerful portion of her lesson as well as the practice she most wants to improve to address her goals of supporting students who struggle with reading. Her planning shows an expectation of a support and develop approach to the observation: showing the meatiest part of her lesson in the area that she thinks she can grow the most. She is hoping for specific feedback on her interactions with individual students and ideas about how she can improve.

Ricki is an assistant principal assigned to observe and evaluate Allison. Rather than sitting in on an entire period, Ricki prefers to do multiple, brief, unannounced visits so that teachers cannot put on a show full of dogs and ponies just because they know she is coming. The evaluation policy requires some announced and unannounced visits, so she asks teachers to send her preferred times for the announced visits.

When Ricki visits classrooms, she brings the state rubric and takes notes on the criteria listed in each row. By keeping her observations focused only on specific rubric criteria, Ricki ensures all teachers are being held to the same standard and that feedback can be linked to actionable next steps for professional development options that are linked to each rubric row (e.g., planning, management, assessment, and so on).

Ricki is applying a measure and sort approach to her observations: trying to collect the most objective, reliable data over time to make the best decisions about teacher quality. When she enters Allison's classroom midway through her lesson, she finds the students reading independently. Some are also writing in their journals, and some are reading next to each other on the classroom rug. Allison is kneeling next to one of them whispering something. No students are interacting, there is no explanation of content, no one states the lesson objective, no group work is facilitated, there is no evidence of active listening, and no expectations are stated. In short,

Ricki sees nothing she can rate on the state rubric. She writes a quick note on a sticky note to Allison telling her she's sorry she got the time wrong and will come back some time when she can catch Allison teaching.

Ricki didn't get her objective, reliable data. Allison didn't get her specific actionable feedback. No one discussed suggestions or resources aimed at instructional improvement. What went wrong?

Both educators had good intentions and were thoughtful about this observation, but each applied a different logic to address what they viewed as the purposes and possibilities of classroom observations.

If their shared goal had been to measure and sort, Allison would have been better off showing Ricki the first part of the lesson, where teacher-directed instructional patterns would allow her to clearly highlight each indicator on the rubric—from stating the lesson objective to facilitating student discussion. Allison may not have gotten feedback in the area she was hoping for, but she would have ensured that her evaluator had evidence she should be sorted positively (e.g., renewed, promoted, tenured). Perhaps Allison's goals for support and development could be addressed outside the evaluation system by a mentor or coach.

On the other hand, if their shared goal had been to support and develop, Ricki might have been better off meeting with Allison before the observation so that she could be sure she understood what Allison was hoping she would observe. She might have consulted or brought an expert in literacy instruction who would have ideas about how to rate and extend specific practices that are not on the rubric, like conferencing with students. Ricki would not have been able to gather objective, reliable data on Allison's classroom that could be compared to data from all of her other observations, but she would have recognized the instruction Allison wanted to show. Perhaps data for comparisons could be gathered during instructional rounds or trend visits instead.

Both approaches are valid ways to engage with the tools and routines of goal setting, classroom observations, and feedback conversations. However, each logic must be used intentionally and separately. Segments of instruction designed to invite support and development are difficult to measure and sort. Evaluation tools designed to measure and sort do not easily generate feedback for support and development.

Using either system of logic only requires a decision, but it is not one that teachers or evaluators can make on their own. Teachers and evaluators are both influenced by their backgrounds, current professional environment, and other reform pressures when they draw upon these logics. This means that different logics may be in play at one time, and that some might be used more often depending on context. For instance, leaders in chronically underperforming districts may naturally select the measure and sort logic more often because they consistently face accountability pressures. Leaders in other districts may naturally select support and develop logics more often to push teachers whose scores are consistently satisfactory. Either way, the teacher–evaluator duo has to be on the same page for evaluations systems to produce any of their intended outcomes.

The success of teacher evaluations does not depend on the decisions of teachers or evaluators; it is an interactional accomplishment between the two. As we note above, this means that the successful teacher–evaluator duo:

1. shares a common logic which guides their engagement with evaluation activities
2. approaches evaluation activities with a common understanding of effective literacy teaching.

Such interdependence is not just limited to observation: it applies to all components of a teacher evaluation system, including goal setting, and the selection of measures for student growth and achievement. So, this book is written for teachers and evaluators to read together, to work toward a common vision of effective literacy instruction and a common understanding of the logics that exist and, at times, compete, within teacher evaluation systems.

Why We Wrote This Book

As former reading teachers, literacy coaches, and current researchers who prepare both teachers and leaders, we have watched the proliferation and reach of this new generation of teacher evaluation policies change the volume and focus of conversations about teaching and learning in schools. This has led us to ask two questions that are the driving forces behind the research, examples, and strategies presented in this book:

1. How can evaluation be implemented as a lever for improving literacy instruction?
2. How can teachers and leaders learn about and advocate for high-quality evaluation practices that support student literacy learning?

In the chapters that follow, we present our answers to these questions. In doing so, we argue that evaluation can indeed be used to support literacy teaching and learning, but only if teachers and leaders have a shared understanding of excellent literacy instruction, and of teacher evaluation in the context of accountability policies. Shared knowledge of both is required if teachers and leaders are to make teacher evaluation work for them.

Without this shared understanding, leaders may struggle to look and listen for best practices in literacy instruction as they observe and rate teachers in their buildings. Teachers may struggle to articulate the intention and value of their practices as they set goals and prepare for observations, and they may feel they have to abandon or hide their best instruction behind closed classroom doors. Both may experience the stresses and controlling aspects of evaluation without a clear link to opportunities for growth that might benefit students.

How to Use This Book

We organize the book into eight chapters on evaluation, literacy instruction, and each component of new-generation evaluation policies. Key questions frame each chapter and are followed by descriptions of scenarios that highlight the importance and complexity of focusing evaluation on literacy instruction. These scenarios are based on common stories that we see unfolding across schools, districts, and states as they tackle new policies. Some happened this way, but others are composites of stories we hear over and over again from teachers and evaluators in different settings. We discuss each scenario in terms of the research and practice principles that could guide teachers and administrators in similar situations. Then, we present how topics tie to the measure and sort and support and develop logics. Finally, we conclude each chapter with a shareable list of key points and a take-and-go activity to share with your professional community.

Though you can read through the chapters in order, we invite you to use the detailed table of contents to find what you need when you need it. For example, you may choose to read Chapter 7 on goal setting prior to setting your evaluation goals in the fall. Or, teachers and evaluators may choose to read Chapter 4 on literate environments in June to plan for next year.

With the goal of increasing communication about literacy in the context of teacher evaluation, this book is designed to be used in multiple ways by multiple audiences:

1. for teachers reading on their own to understand the policy context and to gain ideas to advocate for focused, meaningful evaluation

2. for administrators/school leaders reading on their own to learn what to look for when observing literacy instruction across grades and content areas
3. for teachers to read in grade-level teams, data teams, or professional learning communities (PLCs) to discuss elements of effective literacy instruction and goal setting
4. for leaders in PLCs working to encourage more consistent and thoughtful evaluations that improve literacy learning in their buildings
5. for teachers and leaders to read together, to build a common understanding of literacy instruction and teacher evaluation policy.

Key Points

1. Mixed messages about the purposes and processes of teacher evaluation have made teachers and leaders confused, anxious, and often disillusioned about the entire process of evaluation.
2. For teacher evaluation to be used to improve literacy instruction, teachers and evaluators need common understandings, language, and tools for talking about literacy in the context of teacher evaluation.
3. New-generation teacher evaluation systems invariably contain at least two competing logics: the logic of accountability (measure and sort) and the logic of development (support and develop).
4. The success of teacher evaluations does not depend on the decisions of teachers or evaluators, but is an interactional accomplishment between the two.

Teacher Evaluation Systems

From Policy to Practice

▶ *What do teachers and leaders need to know about policy?*

▶ *How can educators learn about policies to advocate for themselves and their students?*

In the summer of 2015, three years after Connecticut adopted its own version of the new-generation teacher evaluation policies that have swept across the United States, I (Sarah) stood in front of a cohort of eleven teachers in my course on education policy and asked them to describe the strengths and weaknesses of SEED (System for Educator Evaluation and Development), the acronym for the state's evaluation system. I was met with blank stares. Once I spelled out the acronym, two of the eleven teachers said they thought that was the name of their district's evaluation program. The others had never heard of it. It turns out that, in an effort to demonstrate that each district had autonomy to create its own models (once approved), many districts weren't using the state acronym anymore. Some teachers knew it as SEED, others by another name, and some were not sure what their evaluation policies were called or whether they were just part of some other initiative (professional learning communities, walk-throughs, improvement planning). Teachers enrolled in this leadership program were each involved in carrying out aspects of their district's evaluation policy for several hours a week, yet they were confused or misinformed about where it came from (school? district? state?) and what it included (Are our SMART (specific, measurable, achievable, realistic, timely) goals for evaluation or for school improvement? Do observations relate to instructional rounds or teacher evaluation?). The majority of teachers in the room believed that their district had "made up" the evaluation system to make it easier to fire teachers. They lived within accountability and evaluation policies, but lacked fundamental knowledge about them.

Without an understanding of the origins of these policies, which had been shaped by political pressures from the federal level, there was fear and mistrust of the district system. In addition, and perhaps more importantly, there wasn't a clear purpose for engaging with the district's new regulations. This means that educators (teachers *and* leaders) were spending large amounts of time and energy either resisting or complying with a policy they knew nothing about. It also means that teachers, in particular, didn't have the language or context to successfully negotiate, advocate, or use evaluation policies to their benefit.

Making Sense of Policy

Teachers and administrators are sense makers who often make sense of policies differently because they are presented with different information. For example, some central office administrators see the state's complete stipulations related to evaluation, but building-level administrators may only see filtered or edited PowerPoint presentations of key points related to these topics. Teachers see a bite-size subset of this information. In fact, when we interviewed teachers about how they learned about evaluation for the first time, some said they read about it in the local newspaper before they had heard a word about it at school.

Additionally, and maybe more importantly, the differing roles and expectations placed on educators shape their engagement with policy. For example, administrators, especially principals, are treated as middle managers who should contextualize policy (Coburn 2006; Park, Daly, and Guerra 2012). Even though principals may be in charge of their schools, they are not in charge of every decision that affects their schools but rather serve as buffers and translators of policies created at other levels of the administrative hierarchy. Teachers are often cast as rule followers who should comply with policy. This means that teachers may only receive information about how to comply, instead of always receiving information about context and rationale—information to which principals or other administrators may have had access. As a consequence, teachers, and sometimes even school leaders, are often misinformed about policies.

The teachers in my class had more positive reactions toward both the evaluation system and their district after learning about the policy structure. Their district's system made more sense after seeing the state (and even federal) structures that informed its design. That did not mean that they agreed with the policy; in fact, many did not. However, it seemed to be less random and capricious when we discussed its connection to the bigger picture. This points to the way in which policy knowledge can be empowering for educators at all levels. Similar to jazz musicians first learning how to precisely play their scales: Only after fully grasping the structures of an evaluation policy can educators improvise and adjust a new system to fit their needs.

So, how can educators learn about policies? It is vital that educators develop an understanding of the onion layers of the federal, state, district, and school policies (Figure 1.1). Because school systems exist in layers, policies are created and then re-created at each level—with information copied or miscommunicated just like it is in a game of telephone. It is important to note that teachers are the last to receive information. Yet most instructional policies, such as those related to literacy instruction and evaluation, require major shifts on the part of teachers, whether they are involved in conceptualizing the nature of these shifts or not.

Figure 1.2 illustrates how messaging about a schoolwide shift to reading workshop changes from the district to classroom levels, with consequences for the actions of educators positioned in different roles. Similar to the game of telephone, ideas about teaching and learning are distorted and sometimes lost in translation as they are passed through levels of the education system.

For instance, a *superintendent* may frame reading workshop as a way to standardize instructional practice across the district and may invest funds in sending teacher leaders from each school to professional development

FIGURE **1.1**
Nested Layers of Policy

Federal Policy	**Race to the Top Competition** • Criteria award 60% of points for including features of new generation teacher evaluation systems
State Policy	In order to apply for RTTT, states rewrite laws regarding the evaluation of teachers.
District Policy	In order to comply with state policy, districts adopt or create systems, software tools, forms, timelines, training, and expectations for new evaluation systems
School Policy	In order to enact district policies, schools create expectations, procedures, and resources to implement district tools on approved timelines
Individual Actions	In order to follow school expectations and procedures, teachers and leaders use approved tools on approved timelines

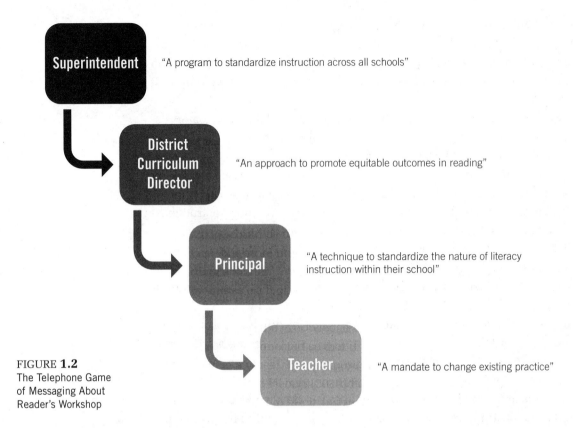

FIGURE 1.2
The Telephone Game of Messaging About Reader's Workshop

Text in figure:

Superintendent — "A program to standardize instruction across all schools"

District Curriculum Director — "An approach to promote equitable outcomes in reading"

Principal — "A technique to standardize the nature of literacy instruction within their school"

Teacher — "A mandate to change existing practice"

on the topic. *Principals*, having met with the superintendent, may frame reading workshop as a technique to standardize the nature of literacy instruction within their school and may create posters and schedules of the workshop routine to display in all classrooms to ensure a standard format for lessons.

At the same time, knowing the research on student-centered approaches to literacy instruction, the *district curriculum director* may frame workshop as an instructional approach to promote equitable outcomes in reading achievement, expecting its formats and pacing to change to shift the needs of particular groups of students. They may prioritize extra training for schools with the largest achievement gaps or highest concentrations of at-risk students. This differentiated support may increase equity but may not support standardization.

Meanwhile, the building-level *coach* of a prioritized school, having met with the curriculum director and knowing the impact of some of the practices contained in a workshop model, may frame reading workshop as a technique to enable students greater access to engaging text. Rather than planning to standardize instruction or prioritize subgroups of students, they may devote time and attention to ordering and organizing books for classroom libraries. For them, workshop is not about standardization or equity, it is about developing a love of reading—and their actions align with this belief.

Finally, *teachers*, having heard from the principal that the school was shifting to a workshop model, see the newly posted schedules and brand-new classroom libraries and draw their own conclusions about what the shift means for their instruction. They may wonder: Is success incorporating new texts into old lesson formats, or spending as much time as possible on independent reading? Is success sticking to the schedule, or differentiating to close achievement gaps?

The irony is that a workshop approach can be used to address each of the goals described above, but not all at the same time. However, mixed messages and multiple intentions for a new initiative are likely to give way to frustration, defeat, and abandonment of this approach for a new one next year. Unless educators at every level have a shared understanding of the focus and intention of new policies, the flavor-of-the-week pendulum of approaches is likely to keep swinging. This is why we believe that all educators have a right and responsibility to knowledge about the policies that shape their work.

Policy Knowledge for Teacher Evaluation

The No Child Left Behind Act (NCLB) was the 2001 reauthorization of the Elementary and Secondary Education Act (ESEA) first passed under President Johnson in the 1960s (see Figure 1.3). When it first appeared, the ESEA was revolutionary both in its reach and its promise to use schools as a place to reduce inequalities. It was the cornerstone of Johnson's War on Poverty and the most prescriptive piece of federal education legislation to date. ESEA established everything from Title I money to fund education programs for low-income students and Title II money to fund teacher professional development, to Title IX money to ensure gender equality in academics and athletics. It was, in theory, the ultimate playing-field leveler.

When NCLB was passed in 2001, it was the first reauthorization in more than a decade. Instead of merely funding programs to level the playing field, NCLB's signature idea was to hold schools accountable for student test scores. Accountability, rather than equality, was the overarching message driving education reform efforts under NCLB. For example, where the original ESEA funded books and reading specialists under Title I, NCLB held schools *accountable* for reading test scores by requiring districts

1965	1968	1975
• Elementary and Secondary Education Act (ESEA) » Funds to schools serving low-income students	• Bilingual Education Act » Funds bilingual programs	• Education of All Handicapped Children Act (PL 94-142) » Requires free and appropriate public education for all
1990	**2001**	**2004**
• Individuals with Disabilities Education Act (1990) » Reauthorizes PL 94-142	• No Child Left Behind Act (NCLB) » Reauthorizes ESEA and the Bilingual Education Act	• Individuals with Disabilities Improvement Act (IDEA) » Reauthorizes IDEA
2007	**2009**	**2015**
• NCLB expires . . .	• Race to the Top Competition announced by executive order	• Every Student Succeeds Act » Reauthorizes NCLB

FIGURE **1.3**
Timeline of Federal Education Policy

to report the scores of each subgroup of students. Furthermore, Reading First, part of NCLB, provided funding in most states for reading coaches who held teachers *accountable* for teaching reading in particular ways, often tightly tied to core reading programs, such as Houghton Mifflin's Open Court curriculum.

NCLB's accountability policies failed to produce large-scale gains in student achievement or equity as measured by the National Assessment of Education Progress (U.S. Department of Education 2015). Reading First also failed to produce large-scale gains in reading achievement and was therefore defunded (U.S. Department of Education 2008). When Obama took office in 2008, NCLB was overdue for reauthorization, but a divided house and senate were as likely to come together to reauthorize major legislation as Haley's Comet is to come two years in a row.

So, the Obama administration took education policy into its own hands with Race to the Top (R2T). R2T drew on the hottest, best-selling education policy report since *A Nation at Risk* came out in 1984. "The Widget Effect," a 2009 report from The New Teacher Project (Weisberg et al. 2009), was an exposé of the current state of teacher evaluation in U.S. public schools. In short, few people were ever evaluated. Evaluations were cursory, meaningless, infrequent, and mostly ineffective. Therefore, the report argued, teachers were retained, promoted, and tenured based on nothing other than a penchant for showing up to work every day. Ineffective teachers, the report suggests, were the root of low achievement and inequity in schools. Teacher evaluation reform was therefore considered a moral imperative. (See Figure 1.4 for links to policy-relevant resources.)

"The Widget Effect" report exposed the absurdity of evaluation policies that lack clear measures, consequences, or impact. It also highlighted a certain brand of research that framed teacher quality as teacher *effect*iveness, with a specific emphasis on the individual effect of a teacher on student achievement. It suggested that individual teachers, not schools, might be held accountable for ensuring student achievement.

1. Executive summary and grant criteria for Race to the Top: https://www2.ed.gov/programs/racetothetop/executive-summary.pdf
2. *The Widget Effect* report: http://tntp.org/assets/documents/TheWidgetEffect_2nd_ed.pdf
3. Expert blog about teacher evaluation, accountability and value-added models: http://vamboozled.com

FIGURE **1.4**
Links to Online Policy-Relevant Resources

It may sound obvious to measure teacher effects on student achievement, but until 2009, only two states did. In fact, some states had laws against the public release of teacher effect data (e.g., Tennessee). The general consensus was that so many in- and out-of-school factors impact a student's test score that pinning variance in student achievement on an individual classroom teacher (or coteacher, or specialist) was nonsensical. There were too many uncontrolled variables. Instead, NCLB required states to measure teacher "quality" by looking at *qualifications* (e.g., degrees, certifications, years of experience).

Measures for calculating an individual teacher's effect on student achievement have been used at the state level in Tennessee since the mid '90s, and Louisiana since the early 2000s, but never for high-stakes decisions and never on a large scale. Legislators did not trust their validity, and statisticians did not trust the ratings of individual teachers, only the average ratings of schools and districts. The formulas were kept secret so that anyone who wanted to conduct or replicate the analyses had to build a complex proprietary model themselves. It has only been in the last twenty years, due to both advances in statistical methodologies and huge investments in district/state data systems, that states and even some large districts have become capable of calculating classroom-level effects on student achievement.

One of the most high-profile methods for calculating teacher effects on student achievement is value-added modeling (VAM). VAM captured the imagination of those who wished it were easier to estimate a teacher's contribution to student achievement despite all of the other possible variables. On the surface, it offered an objective way to measure and sort that balanced the inherently subjective art of observation. Beneath the surface, however, VAM was a method no one understood. That, in fact, was part of its appeal. VAM seemed mystical and, by extension, infallible. It was romanticized as the holy grail of teacher evaluation: the measure we've been waiting for that will save us from the "ineffectives" we didn't know were lurking among our teachers, and the capricious, toothless tools for evaluation we currently use (Gabriel and Lester 2013a).

If you think this all sounds dramatic, you're right. In fact, we found that the media narratives about VAM followed the traditional story structure of romance quests in English literature—complete with heroes, villains, and morality at stake (Gabriel and Lester 2013a). We also found that VAM was used as the excuse for high-stakes policies—the measure that assured policy makers it was OK to link teacher pay, promotion, tenure, and dismissal to student test scores (Gabriel and Lester 2013b). Without it, no one believed test scores could measure teachers. With it, the sky was the limit on our ability to use accountability measures to improve teaching.

The myth of VAM was this: We are unaware of the effectiveness of our teachers, and ineffectiveness may be lurking in every school pulling down averages and making good teachers' jobs harder. The reality was the opposite; even with VAM and high-stakes teacher evaluations, nearly 100 percent of teachers score proficient or above. When measured, very, very few teachers in New York, Tennessee, or Colorado were labeled "an ineffective." In states where VAM formulas required a bell curve where *someone* had to be in the bottom 10 percent and therefore labeled relatively ineffective (e.g., Florida and Texas), evaluations faced a series of high-profile lawsuits.

New-Generation Teacher Evaluation Policies

Instead of legislating a new set of policies and priorities, the Obama administration rewarded states that agreed to enact a particular set of state policies with the R2T grant. Even though only nineteen states won a portion of the $4.35 million in R2T funds, forty-six states applied for them, thus paving the way for changes to teacher evaluation across the nation. Sixty percent of the possible points for R2T applications were related to the development and implementation of a new generation of teacher evaluation policies—those that:

1. evaluated every teacher every year
2. used student growth data as part of teacher evaluation
3. used teacher evaluation ratings to inform human capital decisions (hiring, firing, promotion, tenure)

4. linked teacher evaluation ratings directly to professional development efforts. (This is consistently the only unfunded mandate in teacher evaluation policies.)

Inspired by R2T guidelines, and later guidelines for earning a waiver for NCLB requirements, new-generation teacher evaluation policies share a set of common components: formal and informal observations by administrators, rubrics to score classroom practice, feedback delivered by administrators to teachers, and educator goal setting related to student achievement. These components are measured and weighted differently in each state, but the common formula for an overall teacher rating remains relatively consistent across the country (see Figure 1.5).

Due to the expense and the controversy surrounding VAM, only twenty-four states adopted models that included VAM in particular, but all forty-six states (and DC) include some form of growth modeling, such as the tracking of student learning objectives or calculation of student growth percentiles.

Under the latest reauthorization of ESEA, the Every Student Succeeds Act of 2016, nearly all decisions about teacher evaluation are left to individual states. Therefore, states are no longer required to use the R2T recipe for evaluation systems. However, the recent, significant investment of political and economic capital in new-generation systems suggests that many

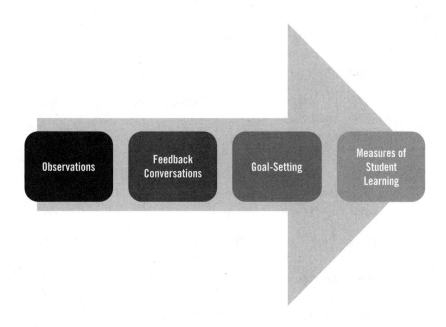

FIGURE **1.5**
Diagram of Evaluation Components

of the core structures are likely to remain in place even if particular tools or guidelines shift over time.

The Mechanisms of Teacher Evaluation

It has now become popular to say that the most important school-based factor in student achievement is teachers. This statement has long been spoken by teachers, researchers, and advocates. However, this statement's place in the mouths of economists and politicians was made possible by VAM—the very same statistical tool that has been the topic of protests, lawsuits, and, shockingly, suicides in New York, Texas, and Los Angeles ever since its inclusion in state teacher evaluation policies (Amrein-Beardsley 2014).

However, as noted previously, the early findings of new-generation teacher evaluation systems indicate that we do not have a sea of ineffective teachers to identify and remove. Year after year, headline after headline reveals that districts, states, and even research funded by the Gates Foundation fail to identify significant numbers of teachers worthy of dismissal (e.g., MET Project 2012). It seems instead that we have a sea of professionals whose instruction is not productively sorted or supported by currently available tools for goal setting, observation, and surveys.

In many ways, the story of teacher evaluation *is* the story of U.S. education policy in the twenty-first century. This is the horse that reformers have bet on, for better and for worse. As educators, we have the right and responsibility to learn about evaluation and make it work in the best interests of our students in our particular contexts.

Here's what it would take to make the evaluation of literacy instruction work for students:

1. Observations have to be tuned to literacy-specific practices and individualized areas for growth.
2. Feedback has to focus on the practices and processes of literacy instruction, not teaching in general.
3. Goals have to be set to inspire, not restrict, ambitious teaching.
4. Student growth measures have to measure what matters most for literacy, not what is easiest to count.

We no longer have the "stick and carrot" of NCLB–era accountability offering rewards or sanctions to schools based on the performance of their students on standardized tests once a year. Under R2Tp, and now the Every Student Succeeds Act, we have ongoing cycles of observation, debriefs, goal setting, and surveys to document weak teachers and build more effective teachers. If we want to work within existing systems to guarantee excellent literacy instruction, we need to build understanding for the systems themselves, and we have choices about how we do this. As we described in the introduction, educators can take a *measure and sort* or a *support and develop* approach to learning about policies. Each approach has benefits and drawbacks, but mixing approaches tends to cause confusion and disappointment.

A Measure and Sort Approach to Learning About Policy

The purest example of a measure and sort approach to policy learning I (Rachael) have ever seen came from a small, well-regarded district in Connecticut. The tightly knit group of central office leaders collaboratively created a set of PowerPoint slides to introduce the new state policy on teacher evaluation based on their own initial training at the state department. They carefully scripted key talking points into the notes of those slides and delivered the file to each building principal. Then, they asked each principal to practice delivering the same information from those slides, using those talking points, so they could ensure all teachers were getting the same message in each building.

When principals "rolled out" the slides and talking points to their faculties during a predetermined window of time (sometime in the first two weeks of September), a leader from central office was present to check that messages were consistent. And, teachers had to fill out an exit slip to demonstrate that they understood the key components of the system. In this district, administrators were monitoring and assessing the introduction and direct instruction of the new evaluation system.

In this view of policy learning, teachers are recipients of policy requirements and the most important aspect of their learning is the accuracy of the message. If there were a bulletin board tracking teacher policy learning in this district, it would be decorated with graphs based on data from exit slips for each building and measures of principal fidelity to the district message. In this way, the central office staff could measure and sort the policy knowledge of its employees.

The upside of this approach is consistency and accountability for a consistent message. However, certain aspects of the system are much easier to describe clearly and measure on an exit slip than others. In our interviews, we found that teachers were very aware of things like the number of required observations, the date on which goals were due, and the percentage of students they had to include in their goals. These numeric indicators of process and procedure had been memorized as mantras (80 percent of 80 percent; 30 percent growth; goals due on October 15).

Yet, district and school administrators had limited time to develop teachers' understanding of the policy's intentions, its origins, and broad goals. Teachers were less clear on what counted as an ambitious goal, what principals were looking for in observations, and why they had to turn in their goals and plans so late in the year. Some, especially those with aspirations toward leadership, took the logistical requirements as a challenge and worked hard to dot every *i* and cross every *t* on time. Others took the overwrought, undercontextualized new policy as a personal affront—further evidence that no one at the state department "has any clue about what it's like to be teaching here in the trenches." Teachers in this district repeatedly remarked that when they had a question that was not addressed by the presentation, no one, not even the central office administrators in the back of the room, had an answer for them. A scripted presentation supports consistency, but may also limit learning.

If the goal is to ensure that a clear, common message makes it through the game of telephone from state to district to school to classroom, district leaders will need to invest significant energy in crafting, developing, and monitoring the message at every phase of delivery. However, as we've found in our work with aspiring teachers and leaders, it is possible that, if state and district leaders were more transparent about the policy and its context, educators would be more willing to follow the policy—for instance, if teachers had structured time to review policy documents, generate questions, and research the aspects of the policy that matter to them. This would create the possibility for teachers to be partners in shaping implementation efforts, rather than being the recipient of decisions made for and about them by others.

A Support and Develop Approach to Learning About Policy

A support and develop approach to evaluation policy learning would give teachers multiple opportunities to hear about and talk about a new policy before implementation. It would uncover the roots of reforms and provide educators with a road map of concurrent policies and initiatives so that it is clear how the new policy fits with efforts. This would require drawing on a range of resources, not a single standardized message, so that teachers and leaders could co-construct what the policy would mean for their school.

In these ways, a support and develop approach would encourage educators to engage with transparent, accessible ideas about policy and would support educators to learn more about these policies to address their concerns, clarify their understandings, and facilitate thoughtful implementation (Hall, Dirksen, and George 2008). This approach empowers teachers and leaders to make a policy work for them, but requires an investment of time, resources, and flexibility.

Key Points

- Similar to the game of telephone, ideas about teaching and learning—in evaluation or literacy—are distorted and lost in translation as they are passed through levels of the education system.
- Educators at every level need to have a shared understanding of the focus and intention of every new policy to implement it responsibly.
- After school/district accountability for student test scores under NCLB failed to improve U.S. schools, policy reports and federal documents framed teacher evaluation reform as a moral imperative.
- All educators have the right and responsibility to explore the ideas and rules of policies related to evaluation and literacy instruction.

Tools to Share

The following tools for Chapter 1 can be found in the appendixes:

- Resources to Support Policy Knowledge
- Process for Becoming Informed About Policy
- Influences on Classroom Practice Discussion Starter

Implementing Teacher Evaluation Systems in Complex Contexts

▶ *How can the time we spend on teacher evaluation add up to positive changes in teaching and learning?*

▶ *What should be prioritized in the time-consuming process of teacher evaluation?*

Distractions

In our interviews and focus groups with several hundred teachers and leaders piloting a teacher evaluation program in Connecticut, teacher and administrator feedback could be characterized as describing one of two simultaneous challenges:

1. too-muchness, and
2. not-enoughness.

Schools are social hubs. They are busy places with multiple missions and layers of initiatives going on at any given time. These initiatives may culminate in events, ranging from a spelling bee or a science fair, to a dental health assembly and a recycling challenge. Add to this rich social and cultural life multiple layers of policies, threats, and expectations related to instruction: curriculum, testing, new students, new passwords, teacher turnover, and copy machines that are basically always jammed. Then enter a teacher evaluation system with five main components, new forms, new meetings, new protocols, and a new set of data to identify, collect, and analyze. The new system is demanding, it's overwrought, and it takes up time and resources that could be allocated elsewhere. *There is simply too much going on.*

At the same time, the culture of teaching in U.S. public schools has historically been to keep the main goal of public schools, instruction, privately conducted by an individual behind a closed classroom door. This is referred to as the "egg crate structure of a school," where teachers are nested inside classrooms with few structures that support meaningful connections between them (Lortie 1975). It is not part of the culture of teaching to talk about your work with any transparency or regularity. Individuals may have to mitigate the social awkwardness of talking about their own teaching with self-effacing comments ("Maybe it's just me, but . . .") or they risk sounding like a know-it-all for broadcasting what they did well. Individuals may also deflect the focus away from teaching and toward students, the principal, or the district ("Marcus just can't sit still during shared reading"; "My district coach didn't deliver my classroom library materials until late October"). Teacher evaluations raise the stakes on conversations about teaching because teachers are going to be rated, compared, and sorted as a result of their instruction. And yet many of us have little practice talking openly, critically, and productively about our own or each other's instruction (Darling-Hammond 2010). We lack common language for thinking and talking about teaching (Ball and Cohen 1999). We lack common visions of effectiveness and safe places to ask, share, and try out new things (Du-Four 2003). *There are simply not enough opportunities to productively talk about teaching.*

Improving literacy instruction may be just one of a flood of initiatives in any given year. So educators are not always talking about instruction when they get together, and, to a certain extent, that is as it should be. It is important to acknowledge that schools have a social, cultural, and political life that can often support, but sometimes eclipse, efforts to improve instruction. This chapter is about naming and handling the topics, tools, and routines that distract us from the fundamental work of talking about teaching and learning. We begin with a few examples of how good intentions do not always lead to productive talk about literacy teaching, and we end with a description of a measure and sort approach and a support and develop approach to maintaining a focus on literacy instruction so that time spent on evaluation *is* spent on instruction.

Tools for Teacher Evaluation

Teacher evaluation systems are designed, in part, to improve instruction. Yet, far too often, we see schools struggling to maintain a focus on instruction precisely because of teacher evaluations. Each component of an evaluation system offers both costs and benefits when it comes to keeping the focus on teaching (Figure 2.1). In other words, each component others both too-muchness and not-enoughness.

FIGURE **2.1**
Costs and Benefits
of Tools for Teacher
Evaluation

Component	Costs	Benefits
Rubrics	• Are one size fits all, so they are not differentiated to account for subject area or grade level • Provide time to learn the language/principles of the rubric	• Provide a consistent framework for observing instruction
Observation Debriefs	• Require coordination of time between administrator and teacher	• Enable administrators and teachers to discuss and reflect upon classroom practice
Goals and Student Learning Objectives	• Emphasize particular forms of assessment • Narrow the focus of efforts in particular areas	• Permit teachers to set focal areas for improvement
Surveys and Whole-School Metrics	• Provide general, undifferentiated feedback	• Provide information on the school as a whole

Rubrics

Rubrics are supposed to be the answer to the problem of no clear vision of effectiveness and no language for thinking and talking about teaching. They articulate a continuum of effectiveness across a number of indicators so that evaluators know what to look for and so that teachers and evaluators have common language for discussing what was observed and what might change. Levels of effectiveness are described in both directions (less and more effective) so that people who do not know a lot about how particular indicators vary or develop can imagine what *should* or *could* be happening in future observations. All of the many pages of gridded text address the *lack of common language and concepts for effective teaching.*

However, rubrics are also designed to apply to a range of roles, grade levels, and content areas, so that everyone is held to the same standard. Unfortunately, this means that all commercially available rubrics are both broad and general. These generic rubrics can lead to generic conversations about teaching that do not get into the nitty-gritty *how*s, *why*s, and *when*s of coordinated opportunities to learn. We worry that this means conversations stay at the 30,000-foot level instead of zooming in to the specific teaching moves used at particular moments and the relationship between the teacher, the instruction, and a certain student or group of students with particular learning needs.

For example, feedback based on rubric language often sounds like: "I noticed you set a clear learning goal and maintained appropriate pacing while teaching in both the whole class and small group format. . . ." It less frequently sounds like: "I noticed that you previewed vocabulary from the shared reading text with a small group of English learners. . . ."

Rubrics for evaluation in their unabridged formats are often many pages long (thirty is the record as far as we know, but most are at least eight pages). There are upward of thirty indicators on most (some have over one hundred). But, as you can see in Figure 2.2, only a small number of indicators focus on instruction in particular, and only a small fraction of those relate specifically to literacy instruction.

The challenge of generic indicators is not unique to reading and writing instruction; all content areas could be evaluated using subject-specific rubrics (and some are even available for this purpose), but most are subjected to a general teaching rubric. If you want to be able to use rubrics to generate specific feedback about literacy instruction, you have to manipulate the tools in specific ways (see Tools to Share for examples).

FIGURE **2.2**
Indicators from Four Common Rubrics

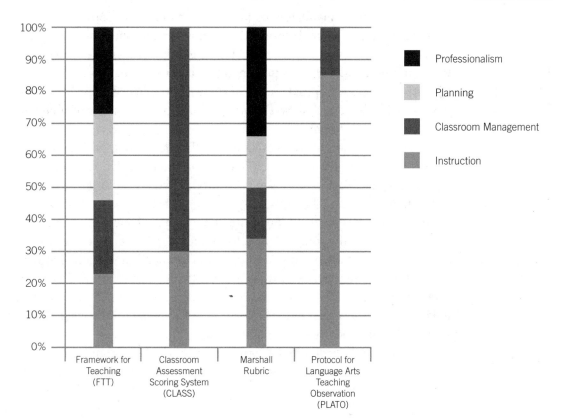

Looking at literacy instruction through a generic lens may oversimplify the processes under observation and therefore inflate scores. For example, teachers in the large-scale Measures of Effective Teaching (MET) Project earned scores that clustered around average ratings on the Danielson Framework rubric with a few earning extremely low or high scores. However, when the same lessons were rated using the Protocol for Language Arts Teaching Observation (PLATO; see Grossman et al. 2013), not a single teacher earned the highest rating in all categories, and most teachers' scores clustered near the bottom of the scale. Similarly, less than 1 percent of math teachers scored at the highest rating on the math-specific Mathematical Quality of Instruction (MQI) tool. The lesson from the MET study is that it is much more challenging and less common to score well on subject-specific than generic tools for teacher evaluation. Some school leaders address this reality by selecting additional rubrics. Others add rows or specifics to their existing rubrics for each of the content areas they observe (see Tools to Share for examples of this).

Observation debrief conversations

Evaluation systems mandate a certain number of debrief conversations or meetings with evaluators before and after observations and goal-setting activities. These are required as part of the evaluation system to create space, tools, routines, and protocols for generating and capturing feedback, reflection, and collaborative problem solving between teachers and evaluators. In other words, they are *designed to address the not-enoughness* of time and ways to talk about teaching.

System designers know that simply calling a meeting will not ensure time is spent engaging in constructive feedback and reflection. Generating high-quality feedback and engaging in productive reflection are complex, interactional accomplishments. They do not just happen because we schedule fifteen minutes for them. So, these conversations come with forms that are designed to guide professionals to include certain content in a certain sequence in their conversation. Filling in the form or following the protocol fills in the *not-enoughness* of ways to keep the focus on constructive feedback and reflection. However, like rubrics, these forms are often unwieldy, long, generic, and unnatural. Moreover, they shape and limit what counts as reflection and feedback (Gabriel in press).

Like scripted curricula, the forms for initial, midyear, and final meetings as well as postobservation conversations are designed to provide foundational support for teachers and evaluators who either wouldn't stay on topic or wouldn't know how to organize a productive conversation without the guidance of a step-by-step form. The presence of a form for every interaction, however, merely adds to the *too-muchness* of paperwork in the business of teaching.

Goals and Student Learning Objectives

As discussed in Chapter 7, goal setting is used to create focus and generate useful data that can guide discussions and action plans across a year. It is used to minimize the *too-muchness* of all the possible things in which to invest energy, time, and resources. Setting goals allows people to marshal shared efforts and pool resources toward a particular end or a collaborative endeavor. In the process, however, goals narrow what matters to whatever is being counted for the goal—thus creating *not-enoughness* when it comes to other data that might drive improvement.

Goals may fill in gaps in collaboration and focus, but system designers know that without strict specifications, people could set any kind of goal they want, and that wouldn't be productive or fair. So, they usually create a process with very specific guidelines, which require new forms and protocols. Goals have to be worded in particular ways, and "draft goals" have to be approved by evaluators before they are "finalized." In some cases, teachers reported going back and forth on the wording of draft goals so many times that their goals weren't finalized until several months into the school year—around the time that some of these goals should have already been met. That also meant that teachers taught for months without an official goal and thus could not have had the proposed benefit of a formal goal in mind for nearly a third of the year. The multistep, multimeeting, multiform process associated with goals setting can contribute to the too-muchness of evaluation systems.

Accountability in Balance

Most schools are operating with layers upon layers of different accountability policies from issues from instruction to attendance—each with their own forms, goals, measures, and outcomes. In this way, education is not unlike medicine at the moment—a 2015 study found that emergency room doctors click a mouse more than 4,000 times per shift to enter information into systems that are designed to increase accuracy, communication, accountability, and therefore outcomes. Most people would agree 4,000 clicks amount to a waste of time, though some would point out that some of those mouse clicks *have* supported the work of saving lives.

It's not the mouse or computer that's the problem, it's the implementation of policies regarding when, why, and how they are used that set or limit the costs and benefits. In a perfect world, the benefits of accountability policies outweigh the costs, but nowhere does this balance happen without intentional efforts to reclaim what matters most about the work they are meant to support.

A Measure and Sort Approach to Implementing Teacher Evaluation Systems

School leaders can take one of two approaches when addressing the dual challenges of too-muchness and not-enoughness. They can take a measure and sort approach that involves working to modify tools and clarify routines so that they run more smoothly and are more user-friendly.

For example, leaders might make a "pocket version" of the rubric that highlights a few key areas for observation. They might choose one focus indicator per observation so they are not attempting to rate teachers on multiple things at once. They may also decide on some goals for the whole school so that teachers are only responsible for coming up with one or two goals instead of three or more on their own.

To streamline paperwork, they might buy into an online system so everything is electronic and centralized (though this can create its own technical difficulties). They may revise forms so that they are not redundant or make them electronic so information is prepopulated.

If they find that certain aspects of the system are taking too much time, despite streamlining or automation, they might use a staff meeting or some professional development time to go over those processes and attempt to optimize them. They might create banks of examples for good goals, reflections, or record-keeping schemes. They might even create incentives or awards for people who comply quickly or consistently to encourage such behavior.

The logic of measure and sort implementation reinforces the tradition of not talking a lot about instruction. Professional development time is used to discuss efficient compliance with processes rather than the instruction these processes are meant to support. Administrator time is focused on streamlining logistics rather than discussing instruction. The benefit of having a bank of prewritten goals is seen to outweigh the cost of not being encouraged to come up with your own. This is because measure and sort logics are based on efficiency—on curbing the too-muchness of new policies. We note that, in contrast to the measure and sort logic, the support and develop logic leaves room for discussing instruction in deeper ways.

A Support and Develop Approach to Implementing Teacher Evaluation Systems

A support and develop approach aims to keep the focus on instruction by changing rather than streamlining the tools and routines. For example, some researchers have embedded language within rubric rows that support a specific focus on literacy instruction and/or the instructional needs of English learners.

Elements 31 and 36 on Marzano's evaluation rubric relate to providing opportunities for students to talk about themselves (31) and for teachers to demonstrate understanding of students' interests and backgrounds (36). According to Lavigne and Oberg de la Gaza (2015), these elements can be *interpreted as* opportunities to make culturally responsive home-to-school and self-to-text connections within a lesson, but the rubric language is not specific about this. In other words, Marzano's original language leaves room for culturally responsive teaching, but does not guide teachers or leaders to focus on this. Instead of leaving it at the original "relate what is being addressed in class to their personal interests" (Element 31), they suggest specifying "relate what is being addressed in class to their language, culture, and personal interests." Similarly, Element 36 already focuses on students' interests and backgrounds, but specifying a focus on language and culture,

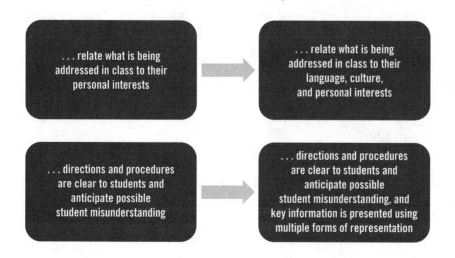

not just "background," guides teachers and leaders more specifically toward culturally responsive practices.

The same can be done with any other general rubric. For example, when the Danielson Framework for Teaching (Danielson 1996) describes criteria for distinguished communication with students (Domain 3a), it is inclusive of but not specific to students who struggle with language or are learning English. Instead of "Teacher directions and procedures are clear to students and anticipate possible student misunderstanding" (Danielson 1996), you could specify that teachers "use research-based strategies to communicate with ELLs" or that they "ensure key information is presented using multiple forms of representation." Alternatively, a separate, specific rubric for culturally and linguistically responsive literacy instruction could be used as a complement or alternative to generic rubrics during some observations or PLC discussions.

To ensure teachers and leaders are focused on shared, research-based understandings of culturally responsive instruction that supports English learners, small groups can meet to examine the specific language of published standards and principles related to research-based approaches in particular. Drawing on existing frameworks and sets of principles ensures the focus stays on targeted, research-based practices where resources and explanations have already been fully developed. Making up your own language may make sense to the few people in the room when it was written, but won't hold up against outside scrutiny or survive the telephone game of communication across a district. The following are some examples of frameworks related to culturally and linguistically responsive instruction that have an identified research base and resources that elaborate, clarify, and demonstrate the principles in action. These could be used as inspiration for infusing specific language into open-ended or generic indicators.

1. The Sheltered Instruction Observation Protocol (SIOP), created by researchers at the Center for Applied Linguistics (Echevarria, Vogt, and Short 2007). It specifies that not only content objectives but also language objectives be displayed and reviewed with students to ensure lessons are planned and executed with language development in mind.

   www.cal.org/siop

2. The Project GLAD (Guide Language Acquisition Design) classroom observation protocol, created by Education Northwest, also focuses on observable features of instruction aimed at supporting language

learners. It includes indicators like "teacher uses strategies that promote comprehensible input" and specifies some of these strategies (such as gestures, appropriate pacing, sketches, and/or realia) rather than leaving them open for interpretation.

https://begladtraining.com/

3. The Culturally Responsive Instruction Observation Protocol (Powell and Rightmeyer 2011) was created by the Center for Culturally Relevant Pedagogy at Georgetown College to identify teachers' use of culturally responsive literacy practices. Instead of indicators aimed at classroom discourse practices in general, it further specifies that teachers provide specifies that "teachers provide opportunities for students to develop linguistic competence and to learn about the situational appropriateness of language use" (Georgetown College 2016).

http://www.georgetowncollege.edu/ccrp/

Building on research that suggests observation systems are biased against certain ethnicities as well as English learners (Lopez 2011), some leaders may choose not to add rows to rubrics, but to elaborate the meaning(s) of existing rows in conversations with teachers. That is, instead of creating more indicators, they generate examples of how teachers might accomplish each generic indicator in their literacy instruction. For example, they might list and describe different configurations for small-group instruction given their particular curricular approach.

The conversations required to map out how each general indicator is accomplished within a literacy lesson and when/how/why this indicator supports good literacy instruction resemble the conversations required in standards-based change movements (Raphael, Au, and Goldman 2009); teacher-led school reform efforts (Stanulis et al. 2016) and other attempts to engage teachers in *envisioning and enacting* a collective ideal rather than complying with one that is handed down. (See Figure 2.3.)

School Rise	Teacher-Powered Schools
http://schoolriseusa.com/	www.teacherpowered.org/
Based on the literacy and school improvement research of Reading Hall of Famers Taffy Raphael and Kathy Au, School Rise employs a seven-step system for teacher-driven, standards-based reform.	This organization supports nearly 100 schools across eighteen states in which teachers share leadership responsibilities and final decisions for the building are made by the teachers collectively rather than by a hierarchy of administrators.

FIGURE **2.3**
Examples of Teacher-Led Reform Efforts

When it comes to debriefing conversations and goal-setting meetings, they might pare down the paperwork by considering that—though the midyear meeting form has fourteen questions on it—it is really about one question: *How are things going?* So that's where the conversation starts. If it stalls or goes off track, prompts from the page can bring it back on track. Otherwise, an open conversation about where things are going is likely to fill in the form one way or another.

Similarly, if the problem with goal setting is that there are goals for evaluation and goals for the school improvement plan; goals for the grade-level team, the department, the school, and the district; goals for attendance and goals for disciplinary actions; goals for turning in paperwork on time; and goals for the number of reams of paper to conserve, aligning initiatives so that a small handful of goals will address all efforts at all levels means more focus and fewer forms. It means turning in the same information to several sources, which doesn't always fit neatly into specialized forms. But the benefit of a small set of meaningful goals is seen to outweigh the cost of imperfect paperwork.

Key Points

- All accountability policies aimed at improving instruction generate activities and paperwork that risk taking the focus away from instruction.
- In a perfect world, the benefits of accountability policies outweigh the costs, but nowhere does this balance happen without intentional efforts to reclaim what matters most about the work they are meant to support.

Tools to Share

The following tools for Chapter 2 can be found in the appendixes:
- Initiative Alignment Tool
- Evaluation Tool Cost and Benefit Discussion Starter

Environments for Effective Literacy Instruction

> ▶ *How do leaders set teachers up for success in their classrooms?*
>
> ▶ *What can teachers and leaders do to build the best environments for literacy learning?*

During his first week of student teaching, a student teacher I (Rachael) supervised burst into our seminar room, slammed the door behind him, and proclaimed: "I just taught the heck out of that lesson!" To which he added, "Too bad the students were all asleep." This bothered me. I couldn't imagine claiming to be successful despite evidence that students weren't paying attention. I always think back to a phrase posted on a sentence strip on the wall of my own student teaching seminar room, which said: "No one's teaching if no one's learning." But it isn't always as simple as teaching = learning or learning = teaching. Sometimes people are trying to teach, or people are trying to learn, but circumstances and materials get in the way. In complex systems like schools, working hard doesn't always work.

That doesn't mean that *teachers* have no effect, some *students* can't be taught, or that *context* excuses bad teaching. It means that all three matter. Before we consider what teachers actually do to create opportunities for literacy growth in Chapter 4, we have to outline the conditions for such opportunities, without which even "teaching the heck out of" things may not add up to learning.

Setting Up an Environment for Literacy Learning

Readers need access to a wide range of texts they can and want to read to develop literacy. This seems like a simple proposition, but it is sometimes challenging to create classrooms and schools where students have regular access to texts they both can and want to read. Some classrooms lack access to appropriately leveled text or to texts that match student preferences and backgrounds (Allington 1977; Cunningham and Stanovich 1997; Worthy, Moorman, and Turner 1999). Some teachers believe or have been told that they must use a certain text whether or not it is appropriate for all the students in the room. Some believe or have been told that texts other than physical books or novels do not count as academic texts. Some administrators believe or have been told that teachers matter more than texts, so teachers should be able to make do with whatever they currently have. Because decisions about classroom texts are often made at a school or district level, texts themselves are part of the context within which instruction takes place. Teachers can spend a lot of time and energy working around contexts that are not supportive of literacy learning by finding their own texts and making up their own activities, or leaders can ensure teachers don't have to by creating environments for literacy learning from the start. Either way, the essential conditions for literacy learning are a joint responsibility.

To ensure all students have opportunities to read something they can and want to read, we argue that three conditions need to be met:

Essential Conditions for Literacy Learning

1. Students must have access to a wide range of text types on a wide range of levels.
2. Adults must consistently demonstrate that they value *literacy*, not just reading or reading test scores.
3. Teachers need time and space devoted to building a literate environment.

Access to a wide range of text types on a wide range of levels

Volume of texts There are studies of the magic number of books required to meet the needs of readers in a neighborhood, classroom, or school library (McQuillan and Au 2001; Neuman 1999; Duke 2000). But middle and high schools host multiple classes in a day, and online resources don't fit the neat and tidy guidelines of 10–25 texts per reader. And it isn't only books that can spark and support reading growth and engagement. Even in elementary settings, it isn't the number of texts that makes a difference: the number of interesting (range of topics and genres), accessible (range of levels) texts make a difference for growth, engagement, and achievement. Investing in renewable collections of paper and digital texts on a wide range of topics and levels is the single most important thing a school can do to create conditions for literacy learning.

The sheer number of texts in a classroom can actually be misleading as an indicator and misguided as an investment. I (Rachael) once conducted an evaluation of literacy programming in a rural school district that had been the target of several recent reform efforts. As a result of reform hopping, the greatest challenge for creating a classroom library was finding new places to store several generations of boxed curricula that they were no longer using. Though many texts existed in the classroom, they were never actually read by students because they were not part of the current curricular framework. In this and other settings, boxes of plastic-wrapped books lined the walls and filled classroom closets, but none of them were read. We found a similar situation in a suburban high school: A cavernous book room served as the permanent resting place for hundreds of volumes that teachers were no longer assigning because they had been replaced by other novels through a series of curricular reforms. Rather than distributing copies to form classroom libraries out of texts that were no longer part of the curriculum, class sets of more than sixty titles simply gathered dust behind a locked door.

Variety of texts Just as we wouldn't expect all children of the same age to be the same height, we shouldn't expect all children in the same grade to have the same reading level. In fact, the range of levels represented in a class of twenty-five students is very likely to expand in later grades as individual differences and differential patterns of practice play out. Some of this is unavoidable because no two children are exactly the same, but some of this variation is the result of limited exposure to a wide variety of texts. As discussed in Chapter 4, all students need access to texts they can read accurately with engagement to develop. This means that teachers need to be able to provide a range of texts both in terms of level or difficulty, and topic, genre, and format.

Gauging the relative level of classroom texts has become big business since the Common Core State Standards popularized the already somewhat popular Lexile analysis tool and required a "staircase of increasing complexity" within texts presented in each grade level. Readability formulas and leveling tools have been around for more than 100 years. Neither are totally adequate ways of judging the difficulty of a text, because relative difficulty depends not only on the text itself but also the reader (their background knowledge, interest, motivation) and the activity (the reason they are reading, what they are doing while reading).

Though we now have lightning fast ways of calculating readability by computer, nearly all readability formulas (including Lexiles) are essentially measuring two factors: vocabulary and syntax—that is, the familiarity/commonness of words that appear in the text and the average length and construction of sentences. Sentences with fewer common words and longer, more-complex grammatical patterns are judged to be more difficult to read. This means that genres often skew readability estimates, as do certain writing styles and text features. For example, informational texts are more likely to use specialized vocabulary, which may be familiar to a given reader, but appears less frequently in print than general terms. Some narrative texts skew estimates because the sentence length of dialogue is usually quite short, so a novel that includes a lot of dialogue, dense and layered as its meanings may be, might appear to be very readable because of its average sentence length. There's nothing easy about a short sentence packed with meaning. There's nothing complex about a long sentence made long because it includes a list of everyday objects. Readability formulas are always only ballpark guesses useful for rating and comparing a huge volume of different texts efficiently.

Their qualitative cousin, leveling systems, use human judgment—often generated by following protocols to generate consensus ratings from panels of teachers, librarians, and other experts—to create ballpark estimates of relative text difficulty. Leveling systems can take many more factors into consideration than quantitative readability formulas because human brains can manage nuances that computers cannot. For example, guided reading levels consider aspects of a text like theme, repetition, assumed background knowledge, density of ideas, familiarity of format and style, and so on. These are still only ballpark estimates based on the consensus of a certain group of raters using a limited set of criteria. So, it has recently become common practice to combine the output of readability and leveling systems into consensus scores. Online readability calculators offer a "consensus calculator" that averages readability ratings from twelve different formulas, and Scholastic BookWizard displays scores from several leveling tools in one text profile. Elfrieda Hiebert, president of the Text Project, has created a Text Complexity Multi-Index (TCMI), which considers the convergence of quantitative indices, qualitative benchmarks, and qualitative dimensions and reader/task factors.

In short, there is nothing terribly scientific or magical about readability or leveling systems. Even the combination of qualitative and quantitative estimates with factors related to the reader and text are really just an effort to combine rough estimations to increase their accuracy. The most responsible way to use them is to take them with a chunky grain of salt as an indicator, not a guarantor, of difficulty. A text that is a guided reading level H should be available to students who are tested around the G, H, or I level. A text that is measured at a Lexile level of 650 should be made available to students who score at *and around* the 650 level, and so on.

Readability and leveling efforts backfire and promote poor reading experiences when they are calculated and applied with a rigidity that their accuracy has not earned. There are too many examples of the "Harry Potter effect" (in which students are able to read far above their expected reading level when they are interested and motivated to do so) and its opposite (difficulty with a text presumed to be easy) because complexity lies between the reader and text, not within the text itself. Because we are always only guessing, ensuring a wide range of available texts is the most responsible way to ensure a positive match between reader and text.

It is also important that students have access to texts that serve as examples that might inspire them as writers. Mentor texts provide models of writing that students can analyze and emulate, while also providing background knowledge that supports content engagement. For example, in a tenth-grade social studies classroom during a World War II unit, students had access to a book cart filled with firsthand accounts from biographies, autobiographies, and collections of newspaper reports. These texts provided access to content and background knowledge for the unit. However, there were also multiple examples of propaganda used during wartime displayed around the room, which served as mentor texts for the propaganda project students completed in which they created their own ads to demonstrate their knowledge of persuasive rhetoric and the issues of the day.

In a fourth-grade self-contained classroom, the classroom library has 10–25 texts per student on a range of levels and topics for independent reading. (See Figure 3.1 for a list of diverse text types.) A book cart from the library also has a set of texts in various formats and genres specific to the current science unit. Along the chalkboard, six copies of personal narratives from various authors are displayed as examples of the genre students are exploring as writers. *In these ways, the texts in the room should reflect and support reading, writing, and content goals.*

FIGURE **3.1**
Diverse Text Types and
Purposes for a Range
of Grades and Content
Areas

Text Types (physical, not including virtual)	Purposes
Magazines	To learn how to make things
Newspapers	To find out how things work
Comics	To learn how to take care of/maintain things
Manga	To connect to things you know
Graphic novels	To find out about new equipment
Manuals	To get examples of new trends
Brochures	To try out a new genre
Information sheets	To connect with a new friend
Annotated diagrams	To discuss with friends
Infographics	To revisit a familiar author
User guides	To laugh
DIY books	To cry
Cookbooks	To feel spooky
Encyclopedias	To get ideas for projects
Newsletters	To get ideas for a trip
Travel guides	To get ideas for writing
Paperbacks	
Hardbacks	

Learning from the texts students choose There are lots of resources pointing teachers toward considering a book's topic and level when making a decision. But a few other features can be equally compelling and important when considering the match between reader and text. These include the book's format, length, and special features (like images, embedded letters, or diary entries, and so on) and its kit of social meanings.

Just like researcher James Gee explained that people have "identity kits" (Gee 2001), books come with a set of social resources—a story about them—in particular classrooms and school settings. Details as simple as knowing who else has read it (the teacher's son at home, an older sibling), or knowing something about who wrote it (a friend of the author of our last book, an author who once visited our school), or the setting it describes (in the time of Davy Crockett, in the Smokies where Dolly Parton was born) form a story about the text that follows it whenever students consider giving it a try.

These kits of meaning about a book are *socially* constructed by the people who think and talk about each text and the images that surround it. That includes the cover as well as media representations of the text in advertisements, films, TV trailers, and so forth. As we know from Harry

Potter, a compelling social toolkit supports engagement and understanding far beyond what we would expect based on measured reading levels. Or, as we know from the kits that surround many high school classics like *The Odyssey*, the chatter that surrounds a book can demotivate students by making it seem dense, irrelevant, and intimidating.

If teachers are considering both the textual and social factors that contribute to a match between reader and text, leaders have to take the same stance. This means that leaders not only would purchase books for teachers, but would devote time for teachers to plan and reflect on the best ways to literally unwrap these texts and fold them into classroom practice. Leaders would not only expect teachers to bless books and bolster their social identity kits, but they would join teachers in doing so—and create forums to do so outside of class time in assemblies, over vacations, online, and during parent events. They would expect teachers to incorporate other texts like magazines, newspapers, brochures, manuals, as well as digital texts in every relevant genre. These texts would not only be present in the building, they would be present in conversation, visibly in use. If literacy is central to your mission as a school, then literate practices—reading, writing, and talking about texts of all kinds—have to be central to your routines and activities.

Values that create literacy-focused environments

It is not enough to make text available if messages about text in the building deter teachers and students from fully engaging with them. For example, I (Rachael) interviewed a group of middle school students who attended a school that used the Accelerated Reader (AR) program to organize and track students' independent reading. The school's interpretation of the program included using the online assessment to identify a student's reading level, and then only allowing the student to read texts on that level (nothing easier or harder). In addition, students could only read one of the fiction or nonfiction trade books that were included in the program (nothing from home or the library) to earn credit for reading. When we asked students about their reading habits, many of them told me they did not read outside of school. When I asked if they read magazines at home, almost all of them said yes.

Why would students claim not to read if they do read magazines? Because school policies about what counts as reading had created a narrow view of reading, one that students were not interested or motivated to engage in outside of prescribed times, and one that did not include a range of text types. Though AR offers some helpful tools for tracking progress and motivating independent reading, it can be implemented in ways that severely limit access to texts and students' sense of themselves as readers.

Students are not the only ones constrained by school policies about what counts as reading. Though many classrooms do make use of nontraditional texts like graphic novels, comics, pamphlets, and magazines at some point in the year, many fail to make texts of multiple levels available to students on a regular basis. Adults (including teachers) often question the legitimacy of anything outside of leveled paperbacks and classic hardbacks. Often, the most useful, compelling, accessible texts in and out of school are not bound in book form. These have to be available, but they also have to "count."

As researcher Linda Gambrell would say, adults have to "bless" such texts—mark them as legitimate for school—by using them, displaying them, and inviting them and acknowledging their uses in and outside of classrooms (Gambrell 1996). Students can participate in book-reading challenges, but they can also participate in current events challenges, weather report marathons, and recipe bake-offs: productive, community-building activities in which texts play a central role.

Many teachers believe it is their job to expose all students to a certain set of key texts in each grade. Many also believe that learning is not cohesive and coherent if everyone is reading their own text. Therefore, there are many schools where multiple texts exist but go unread, because teachers and/or administrators only assign and talk about a single whole-class text at a time. In these cases, teachers' own beliefs or fear of administrative reprisal keeps them locked into discussing a small set of predetermined texts in class.

Individual differences in development and interests mean that it is nearly impossible for a single class text to provide optimal support for the literacy development of a classroom full of students. Yet it is very common for classrooms to rely exclusively on a class set of novels or textbooks for instruction. To be clear, there is value in having a single class text for information and discussion at some points throughout the year. These can serve as anchors, touchstones, and shared experiences that enrich literacy development. There is, however, a problem with *only* having one class text available for information and discussion because this inevitably means unequal access to both content and literacy learning.

For example, if I pick any three students from my first class of seventh graders in Washington, DC, I'm likely to find that they are measured as having three different reading levels and three different sets of interests, backgrounds, and motivations for reading (Figure 3.2). Given ten minutes to read an article, one may read the entire thing and go back to reread a paragraph of interest because they care about the topic.

The second might read it through, but miss some details because the topic is new to him, and not reread sections because he is not motivated to do so. All of this counts as supportive, optimal practice because he is reading it with near 100 percent accuracy, thereby solidifying and extending what he knows about words, word meanings, and written messages. If either of these students comes to a word they don't know, they are likely to make a good guess and incidentally learn a new word. This high-success reading experience supports more high-success experiences because students can solidify and extend reading skills and strategies, which builds confidence in reading ability (Stanovich 1986). The student well matched by interest may even come to associate reading activities with interest, curiosity, and engagement, which builds motivation for reading in general.

The third student might read part of the article, misread a few of the words, and be slightly confused about the message because she read it inaccurately. Not only is this student exposed to less text, with less comprehension, she is not extending what she knows because she can't make good

FIGURE 3.2
Differential Reading Practice for Seventh Graders

	Reader A	Reader B	Reader C
Fluency and accuracy	Reads grade-level texts at 75 words correct per minute	Reads grade-level texts at 100 words per correct minute	Reads grade-level texts at 125 words correct per minute
Motivation	Will read when asked	Dislikes reading	Enjoys reading
Background knowledge	Knows a lot about bikes, likes fiction	Knows a lot about cars, likes nonfiction	Knows a little about bikes and cars, likes nonfiction
Given ten minutes to read a narrative story about a boy riding a bike	750 words of engaged fiction reading	500 words of interrupted, disengaged reading	1,500 words of engaged fiction reading
Given ten minutes to read a newspaper article about new kinds of bicycles	750 words of engaged informational text reading	1,000 words of engaged informational text reading	1,500 words of engaged informational text reading
Outcomes	Slow but steady progress	Around the same as lower-performing peers	1.5–2 times the progress of peers no matter the text

inferences about unknown words or new concepts. More importantly, she is engaged in a reading task where she does not experience success, which makes it less likely that she will have the interest and confidence to sustain her effort, and more likely that she will associate this feeling of confusion or boredom with reading in general.

Cycles of reading success and cycles of reading failure are always at work both at a micro level within a single lesson and a macro level over months and years of reading experiences. In other words, if you do not plan to differentiate texts for students at some point during the day, student learning will differentiate itself and some students will thrive where others struggle to survive.

Teachers who exclusively use single, whole-class novels without incorporating choices, multiple levels, or multiple text types often feel constrained by school policies that privilege a prescribed curriculum or administrators who hesitate to embrace nontraditional texts. Particular approaches to ensuring choice and variety will be discussed in Chapter 4. But for teachers to make use of these important tools, they have to work in a school context that allows different texts at different levels to count as real reading and one that allows multiple texts to be used as part of instruction.

Practices that demonstrate our values Valuing literacy is such a simple idea that it is easy to imagine it is happening even when it is not. Take two reading assemblies at schools that both claim a focus on reading as part of their core missions. They each schedule precious time for a forty-minute all-school assembly to kick off summer reading.

The Blue School Assembly begins with a student-read poem, features a local author, and includes previews and videos about the texts on this summer's list compiled by teachers, former students, and parents. The assembly ends with information about prizes and how to track and earn points for summer reading punctuated by contributions from the cheer squad. Students are given a free copy of one of the summer books wrapped in a T-shirt that has quotes from these books in conversation with one another on the back.

Literacy—not books, not reading, not reading scores—is at the center of this event. Anyone watching would know that reading, writing, and talking about text are part of the core mission of this school.

The Red School Assembly begins with the cheerleaders chanting the three-digit number that represents the school's average reading score. The main address is given by the principal and includes slides showing the recent uptick in scores, punctuated by cheers and applause from the audience as each grade's progress is displayed. The assembly ends with information about prizes and how to track and earn points for summer reading punctuated by contributions from the cheer squad. Students are given T-shirts that say "all means all" and "100 percent proficient!" on their way out.

Reading scores—not books, not reading, and certainly not literacy in general—are at the center of this event. Anyone attending this assembly would know that increasing scores is part of the core mission of this school. Both schools had invested time, energy, and resources in a literacy-related assembly, but only one had kept the focus on reading in a way that might build readers.

Time and space to build literate environments

Schools differ widely in their capacity to quickly and responsively offer access to text. Some teachers have full autonomy with classroom purchases and freedom to sign up for online accounts connected to free or paid subscriptions. Some teachers have to request permission to create online accounts and send multiple emails, reminders, and follow-ups to track down orders.

One of the most helpful things administrators can do is take the guesswork out of access to text so that teachers know what their options are and what processes are needed to obtain access. This means maintaining a public list of existing resources and clear procedures for requesting new or additional materials. It also means planning for reading materials to be used, loved, and shared—which often means they may need to be replaced. Administrators who save 5 to 10 percent of their allotted budget for purchases to replace texts students have used, lost, or otherwise redistributed ensure there is always a steady supply.

Likewise, teachers and leaders who facilitate trading, sharing, and/or redistributing resources between grades and classrooms ensure that a finite amount of text resources reach more students. Traveling book carts, a book swap box, and community book drives are all low-cost, successful ways to spread resources throughout the building and ensure students have access to texts they can and want to read.

There are so many vast sources of texts online and from educational publishing companies that it can be difficult to judge the quality and utility of the texts they include. When purchasing materials or access to online materials, it is important to consider not just the quality of the texts, but the quality of the experience that surrounds those texts. For example, it is a good sign when a package includes examples of high-interest, leveled texts. However, if the package limits student access to texts at their tested level, or limits their engagement with such texts by requiring them to answer low-level questions before they move onto the next passage, the package might be sending disengaging messages about what counts as reading that contrast with the messages you work hard to send in your school community. If, on the other hand, students have choice of a range (even if a limited range) of texts and can engage with texts for a range of purposes (they are not locked into a prescribed sequence of activities), teachers may be able to fold these texts into responsive, individualized instruction or practice.

Trading and swapping schemes also have the added benefit of bringing new options into view periodically. Studies of magazine reading habits and our own experience with the excitement of getting mail—even junk mail—tell us that there is an immediacy and a novelty effect when new materials enter the room (Gabriel, Allington, and Billen 2012a, 2012b). People are most likely to read a magazine the day it arrives (though many also pick them up later). And students are more likely to gravitate toward new arrivals in the classroom library, especially those that have been mentioned or highlighted by someone they know.

Though many of these strategies require no additional funding, they do take time to organize. School leaders need to recognize and create space for teachers, librarians, specialists, and/or volunteers to maximize the textual resources in the building. They must also make procedures for securing online access clear and user-friendly so that teachers don't spend weeks requesting passwords to log on and can take full advantage of the growing supply of high-quality, leveled text online.

The need for time and space: Two examples Northeast High School has two separate loading docks where newly ordered school materials can be delivered. Perhaps this is why it took nearly four work days to track down a $30,000 shipment of books for classroom libraries bound for the ten English department classrooms on the third floor. How do you lose fifty cardboard boxes of books in one building? You order them at the same time as all orders for all departments for a school of over 2,000 students.

Once we found the fifty boxes of books bound for classrooms, we had to:

1. Coordinate their transfer up to the third floor.
2. Open every box.
3. Cross-check the number of copies included for each title with our order.

4. Enter each title into the bar-coding system and apply a bar code sticker to each book.
5. Check that it scanned correctly.
6. Sort the books into classrooms sets with 2–3 copies per book per classroom.
7. Find the box of cart parts that had recently been delivered to the main office by mistake.
8. Screw together ten brand-new metal carts that would convey the books to the classrooms while leaving them mobile for later swapping and sharing.
9. Email teachers to let them know which cart was theirs.
10. Watch as the carts eventually made their way into classrooms for use.

Despite the enormous financial investment in literacy, the enormous professional investment in selecting and ordering hundreds of new titles for use in classrooms, and the good intentions of high school teachers aiming to increase access to texts students can and want to read: *texts* and *values* aren't enough. We needed time and space to build a literate environment out of its physical components—in this case: books, bar codes, and carts.

And then, we needed readers. We needed time for teachers to see the books, pick them up, flip through them, notice what was there, wonder about what wasn't, read a few pages, find the titles they would "bless" publicly with a book talk, and find the titles they would save for particular students they had in mind. All this also takes time and space—sometimes weeks of it.

In some buildings, book processing and distribution isn't anybody's job, and there may not be room for it in the jam-packed days of classroom setup before school opens. This could mean highly trained literacy specialists spend several weeks of their time organizing materials, instead of doing any other task. It could also mean a team of teachers tackles the challenge, which means time originally allocated to some other worthy activity is sacrificed to make room for this expression of values and investment in text. Once in a while, an individual takes this on during after-school hours, staying late or coming in early and on weekends to preview and sort. This means the individual teacher knows the system and the collection well, but may not position the whole faculty to take full advantage of the resources someone sacrificed personal time to organize.

Often, it just means the books stay in boxes. Some for a few weeks, sometimes for several years. Hidden away in the closets or back shelves of many school buildings are reading materials still swaddled in shrink-wrap, out of view and out of grasp of the students they were made for. Part of this is explained by curriculum and initiative overload and the distribution of unsolicited samples, but part of it is evidence of the lack of time and space to build literate environments out of available physical materials.

At Southwest Middle School, the reading teacher's classroom was actually a retrofitted closet. This posed some challenges for creating a welcoming environment, but had the added benefit of a backdoor connection to the high school's ancient book room. What the reading teacher lacked in square footage, she gained in full access to stacks and stacks of texts—many never opened—that she could use to build a library whose range rivaled any in the district.

Instead of a wall of glossy, uniform books, all from the same publisher, in color-coded bins, her closet room was a mishmash of hardcovers, magazines, softcovers, anime, comic books, textbooks, and pocket paperbacks of all shapes and sizes from all different publishers. It was totally inviting.

Students were put to work sorting their own libraries, previewing titles for potential inclusion, discussing the benefits of organization by author or genre. They wrote rationales for the inclusion of some texts over others, debated the value of different titles, voted some out of the room. Their eyes and hands were on every one of those books resurrected from the book closet and displayed on the one bookcase that could fit in the closet room for reading. This environment was not the result of a recent financial investment in texts. It was the result of one teacher's *time and space* to create an environment that represents how much she *values* critical engagement with a wide range of text.

Receiving, sorting, learning, sharing, and using textual materials is time and thought intensive. Yet teachers often feel pressured to use certain texts or avoid others. They are told that they must be using the brand-new set when members of the board come visit the school on their tours. Or, they are told what needs to be on display in their rooms, whether or not these texts are actively in use by their students. They need time and space to make decisions about what they include and how in literate environments that are based on students as readers and not on logistics and politics.

As with fresh ingredients destined for a recipe, books have to be selected, processed, and organized with care—not to create beautiful displays, but to ensure that powerful experiences await the readers who eventually take them up and read them.

A Measure and Sort Approach to Creating Environments for Literacy Learning

A measure and sort approach to ensuring access to texts students can and want to read might simply mean counting the texts available in a classroom and including choice of reading material as a checkbox on walk-through and extended observation forms. In fact, "book audits" and text inventories have been used in research and evaluation efforts for more than fifty years.

One year, we consulted on an initiative that involved the purchase of new books for a ninth-grade academy. A librarian used the *New York Times* best seller list to create the book order, which resulted in several thousand dollars' worth of books many adults would probably like to read that were too long, difficult, or mature for most ninth graders. These beautiful, expensive, hardcover copies of popular adult titles sat on shelves without being cracked by student readers. After gathering dust, they were moved to a bookroom to be stored away from the glaring sunlight of classroom windows. Although the funding for these books sent a positive message to students and teachers that books matter, the kinds of books that "mattered" under this scheme were largely out of reach for student readers. So their uses (or lack of uses) sent an entirely different message about the role of texts in literacy instruction.

On the other hand, we have worked in some classrooms that have very few texts, but each text is obviously well loved. They include dog-eared copies that are consumed, discussed, and shared by students on a regular basis. Sometimes these well-loved texts are nontraditional text types like magazines, guidebooks, comic books, brochures, or pamphlets. Sometimes classrooms access text using laptops or other devices so there are few physical copies to count. So, we know that simply counting the number of books available may be a poor indicator of access to texts students can and want to read. The question should not be: Are there any texts here? It should be: How are texts here used?

A measure and sort approach would calculate access by observing students in action and counting the frequency with which students engage with text along with the range of types, topics, and levels that can be found in use.

A Support and Develop Approach to Creating Environments for Literacy Learning

A support and develop approach to ensuring texts students can and want to read are both valued and available means recognizing two truths about engaged reading:

1. *It's personal:* We can never predict what text will be the watershed text that carries outsized significance for readers at a particular moment in their lives. So, we have to hedge our bets by increasing exposure to choices, options, and possibilities, but we also have to model the pivotal importance of texts in our work and lives.

   I saw the clearest example of this when observing a student engaging in one-to-one reading instruction in a self-contained special education classroom. As an eighth grader, he was still struggling with texts written on a first-grade level. He dutifully labored through flash cards of sight words, short passages of leveled text, and short-answer questions using an ornate system of behavioral motivators, breaks, and incentives. One of the incentives was ten minutes in the break room, which contained two yoga balls and a box of fun texts—including two books of Garfield cartoons. The quiet, reluctant reader who sighed and needed prodding for each individual word at the reading table read every speech bubble in different voices, with all the sound effects and punctuation, and laughed out loud at what he read on page after page of the Garfield book.

   There was a total transformation in emotion, affect, engagement, but also proficiency when the text and setting changed. This student accurately and fluently read words and sentences that he had stumbled and given up on just moments before. When I wondered aloud how the well-loved Garfield texts had found their way into the break room, I learned that the teacher brought them from home because her own son had loved them, and she thought someone else might too.

   This student's love of Garfield books put his strengths, interests, and motivations as a reader into sharp relief. Some observation, some questions, and some experimenting showed us that the short pieces of text, picture support, humor, and cause-and-effect structure were both strengths and interests of his in this and other texts. His teachers were able to use patterns of engagement across different reading experiences as evidence to rethink choices for his one-to-one lessons, and they began to see steady gains. It won't always be Garfield, but it will always be something. The wider the range of options, the more likely all students will find their fit.

2. *It's social:* We are each other's reasons for reading. The number one reason adults read nonrequired texts is the recommendation of someone they know or the chance to discuss the text with someone they know.

As a form of communication, the written word is fundamentally about connection, and yet—in school settings—we often read in disconnected ways without the opportunity or expectation of sharing texts and talking about what we read. Choosing a "just-right book" based solely on the measured level match may isolate readers by connecting them with texts no one around them is reading, increasing the disadvantage of struggling readers compared to their peers. Reading for twenty minutes at home each night for homework and writing reading responses in our own private journals are all practices that *can* add up to literate lives, but they won't if we don't have anyone to share our reading with.

Even the eighth-grade student slogging through his reading program to read a few pages of a Garfield book wanted to share his reading with someone else. In the five minutes I watched him reading, I heard him say, "Look at this, would you look at this!" multiple times, rereading a favorite part so others would hear it too.

A support and develop approach involves building or displaying resources based on observations of students' responses and connections to text, so that collections are shifted and reshaped each year to fit the readers they are meant for.

Key Points

- Texts: Classrooms must have access to a wide range of text types on a wide range of levels.

  » A variety of texts can be beneficial because students have a range of reading levels, interests, and experiences.

  » Books are necessary, but not sufficient, resources for effective literacy instruction.

- Values: Adults must consistently demonstrate that they value *literacy*, not just reading or reading test scores.

  » Texts of all types and levels must count as real reading.

- Time and space: Leaders should protect time and space for educators to organize and use a variety of texts.

Tools to Share

The following tools for Chapter 3 can be found in the appendixes:

- Things to Look For/Questions for Discussion About Environments and Resources for Literacy in Your School
- Questions for Discussion About Classroom and School Libraries
- Cycles of Reading Success/Failure
- Allocated Versus Actual Timekeeper
- Criteria for Quality Sources of Online Texts
- Sources of Leveled Texts Online
- Coaches as Partners in Evaluation

Effective Literacy Instruction

▶ *What are the active ingredients that make literacy instruction effective?*

▶ *What does each look like in a classroom observation?*

Literacy instruction presents a special case for teacher evaluation because there is such range and division among practitioners and researchers about what constitutes best practice. Teachers and leaders hold deep-seated beliefs about what counts as appropriate and effective literacy instruction. Ideas about teaching and learning contained in evaluation systems may align or clash with an educator's perspectives on literacy. In the face of passionate arguments for contrasting approaches to literacy instruction, it is easy to become brittlely narrow in focus, or overly liberal—accepting any-and everything. The goal of this chapter is to highlight the non-negotiables of literacy instruction that must be in place, even if they may at times be intangible or difficult to observe.

The first questions I (Rachael) ask when I walk into any literacy classroom at any grade level are:

- What are they reading?
- What are they writing?
- What are they talking about?

If there is no reading, writing, or talking going on in a literacy classroom, the students are doing something other than literacy at the moment, in which case the question becomes:

- Will this activity efficiently lead to reading, writing, or talking about text?

How Teachers Use Time

There are lots of things that might be happening besides literate practice (reading, writing, talking about text) that may eventually support literate practice (taking out materials, listening to directions, and so on), but they have to actually lead to practice for literacy learning to occur.

In other words, while all teachers spend some time on community building, logistics, and incidentals, exemplary teachers routinely spend 80–90 percent of allocated time with students engaged in literate practice, while a teacher next door may spend far more time on "literacy-related" activities and fail to get to the literacy efficiently enough for growth (Allington and Johnston 2002).

In a short observation or walk-through, you may not expect to see reading, writing, or talking about text for a certain percentage of your visit, but asking yourself (and students) how the action you observe *will lead to* literate practice will help you predict the overall pattern of how this teacher uses time better than looking at a schedule or lesson plan.

For example, in two fourth-grade classrooms next door to one another, I watched the same scripted lesson being taught by two teachers with the same years of experience, the same curriculum and materials, and similar populations of students. Both classrooms paused for discipline incidents, took time to engage in an organizing procedure, and spent time listening to multiple announcements over the PA system. Still, in one room, the students were either reading, writing, or talking about text for nearly sixty-eight minutes of the ninety-minute period. Clear goals for reading and audiences for writing were discussed throughout the period so that students had a reason to initiate and persist with reading and writing tasks.

In the other room a combination of long explanations, disciplinary standoffs, disorganized materials, teacher anecdotes, and student questions left only about thirty minutes for literate practice—less than half the allocated time in the scripted lesson. When this classroom veered off-script, it was not to set or reinforce reasons for reading and writing, it was to reinforce classroom rules and discuss how to redo work. In other words, when students weren't reading, writing, or talking, what they were doing was not very likely to lead to literate practice. With half the opportunities to learn, we wouldn't expect the students in the thirty-minute room to do as well as their peers who had 50 percent more practice (Figure 4.1).

Researchers have literally sat in the back of classrooms with stopwatches keeping track of the time spent on various classroom tasks. However, we do not recommend that evaluators do this because effectiveness in teaching is not about the minutes. It's about the volume of opportunities to develop literacy,

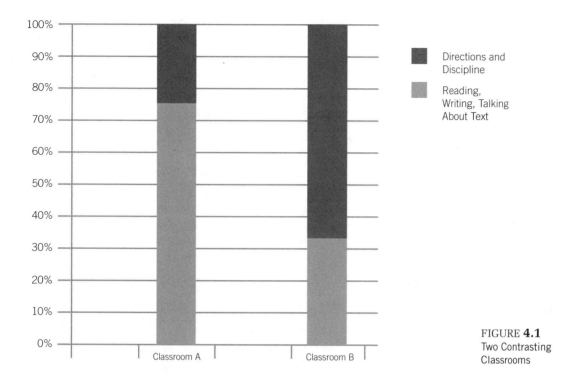

FIGURE **4.1**
Two Contrasting
Classrooms

each of which requires a coordination of time, materials, and instruction. In other words, not all practice opportunities are equal. A few active ingredients are needed to make student growth curves rise as a result of engaging with literacy instruction. As in baking, the mere presence of active ingredients (like baking soda) does not guarantee success, but success is unlikely without them.

Active Ingredients

1. Reading accurately with a purpose
2. Writing with a purpose and audience
3. Talking about text with teachers and peers
4. Discussing models of fluent reading and expert writing
5. Interventions that support individuals and focus on meaning.

Reading accurately with a purpose

As with exercise, we know that there is such a thing as too easy, too hard, and "just right" for growth. This has led to the popular use of ideas like the "Goldilocks principle" or "five-finger rule" for text selection, in which students are instructed to find a book that they can read with at least 95 percent accuracy by counting the number of unfamiliar words on a page of text (5 per 100). Though widely accepted as a tool for selecting independent reading books, there is less consensus about how texts might be selected for whole-group reading—with some people arguing that challenge and complexity are necessary and others advocating for texts that match the readers and not the grade.

A range of studies have confirmed that the volume of accurate reading is directly correlated with achievement during regular instruction and the amount of growth in intervention settings. As Allington, Billen, and McCuiston (2015) describe, the ways we measure text difficulty (or now: complexity) has changed over time, but the central premise that accurate reading matters has remained a constant in studies of the last fifty years. Here are just a few examples of how studies have demonstrated that accurate reading matters over time:

- Linnea Ehri and colleagues (2007) compared the reading growth of first graders involved in a tutoring program that required reading independent-level materials with paraprofessionals compared to small-group instruction from a reading specialist using instructional-level materials. Those tutored using independent-level texts outperformed those reading instructional-level texts in small groups despite their access to a certified reading specialist.
- Elfrieda Hiebert (2005) compared the fluency growth of students who engaged with repeated reading of grade-level materials from their classroom, or passages, and content-specific passages that were controlled to limit the number of unknown words. Both groups made more gains in fluency than a control group that did not do repeated readings, but the group that read texts with greater accuracy (controlled for unfamiliar words) made significantly more growth than the group with uncontrolled text.
- O'Connor and colleagues (2002) compared the efficacy of a reading intervention using texts drawn from students' classrooms versus the same intervention using texts that tutors matched to each student's reading level. Though both groups made more growth than those not receiving any intervention, the reading-level-matched group made significantly more growth than the group using classroom texts.
- Anderson, Evertson, and Brophy (1979) found that the number of errors second-grade students made during classroom oral reading was negatively correlated with their achievement compared to peers who

read orally with fewer errors in class. This difference was less substantial for fifth graders, indicating that oral reading accuracy may be most important for beginning readers.

There are also studies that demonstrate growth is possible when using instructional or even more challenging texts. However, such growth has only been identified in programs that are designed to provide significant support before and after reading, as well as intensive assistance (by peer or teacher) during reading (Stahl and Heubach 2005; Morgan, Wilcox, and Eldredge 2000). In studies of adult readers, psychologists have found that interest mediates the effect of text difficulty such that readers are able to understand and remember more challenging texts even better than easy texts because the challenge increases attention, but only if they are intrinsically motivated to do so (Fulmer et al. 2015).

At the most basic level, reading development requires *practice* to solidify skills and strategies and *exposure* to new words, structures, and ideas to increase one's vocabulary, understanding of text structures, and background knowledge. This requires a balance of challenge and ease that is difficult to achieve in a single text or for large groups of students at a single time. To ensure all students have *some* exposure to text they can read accurately, teachers either provide two or more options of texts to read, use multilevel or multimodal text sets, or allow students to independently read self-selected texts to ensure a match between reader and text for some part of the lesson.

If every classroom observation involves students reading the same text, a leader might ask when students have the opportunity to read on their own level. If the answer is never or only for homework, then a key ingredient is missing from this lesson. Though students can read on their level independently, independent reading should sometimes happen in class so that teachers can observe and coach while it's in progress. Otherwise, they are only engaging with students around the *result* of independent reading (a log, response, or summary) instead of the *process* of independent reading.

A leader might also ask what supports are in place for students who cannot read the class text with accuracy, and whether these supports are likely to allow students the same opportunities to develop content and literacy knowledge as their peers. These should be honest open-ended questions, not quizzes with a short list of known answers. Teachers, especially content area teachers, often have thoughtful and creative ways to support students' understanding and use of texts at and above their independent levels. So, asking about supports is as much about ensuring teachers *have* a plan for differentiation as it is about helping administrators gather practices to share with those who don't.

Asking also tells you why differentiation is happening or not. If an administrator knows that a teacher's intention to differentiate is limited by resources, he can focus on identifying such resources. If, on the other hand, an administrator sees teachers avoiding differentiation altogether, he can focus on supporting the teacher's knowledge and skills in this area.

Motivation to read We often think about motivation like a physics problem: There is an object that needs to be moved, inertia presents a challenge for initiating that movement, so some kind of force is required to accomplish the move. There are two levers that educators can pull to exert force on that object and make it more likely that inertia will be overcome by movement: confidence and desire. Offering a choice makes use of both levers at once. When students are invited to choose between two or more options of what to read, they are likely to choose the text that interests them the most, and the text they are most confident they can read. It follows that students will read more when they have chosen an accessible text.

Motivation theorists challenge us to complicate this mechanical understanding of motivation by considering a few more factors that have been found to contribute to engaged reading (Klauda and Guthrie 2015). To imagine the forces at play, it is helpful to think about motivation as if it is fuel in a fuel tank. Some students may come in with a certain level of "fuel" from their own *intrinsic* motivation to engage with particular literacy tasks. They may also (or not) have a sense of the *value* of the reading/writing task based on how the teacher framed the purpose for reading. To this level of motivation they may (or may not) add a sense of *self-efficacy*—the confidence that they can do this literacy task successfully. Finally, they may (or may not) come with *social* support for reading—access to social reasons to read and social identities as readers that support their engagement. Each of these sources of motivation adds to the level of fuel driving students to initiate and sustain their effort and engagement.

As students encounter challenges, their levels of motivation may decrease as this fuel is used up. As they encounter instruction that supports each of these factors, they have the opportunity to add fuel and top up their supplies. In this way, literacy instruction can either be additive or subtractive: it might fuel engagement by considering *intrinsic interest*, *value of the task*, *self-efficacy of readers*, and *social support for reading*, or it might burn up any existing motivation by failing to account for these factors. Readers with a history of successful literacy experiences often come with fuller tanks to begin with, and thus are less impacted by instruction that does not offer additional fuel. But students who are not intrinsically interested, or confident, need the addition of supportive contexts for engagement to initiate and sustain efforts.

Purpose for reading To fuel motivation and ensure successful reading experiences, students need a purpose for reading every single time they read. The purpose can be short or long term, formal or informal, but it has to exist. Otherwise students will be forced to use motivation reserves to fuel their engagement, and they may pay attention to all the wrong things. For example, if you tell a classroom full of students to read a chapter of a novel at the end of class, but tell one third to read it as if they are movie producers trying to find the best scene for a trailer, one third to read it as if they are actors preparing for a role, and one third that they can go to recess as soon as they finish, they will each pay attention to different things. The producers will attend to the climax scenes and not even notice the characters' names, the actors will pay attention to physical features and details and emotions, and the third group will be watching the clock most of the time, missing most of the details. Likewise, if you assign a chapter of a science textbook with no particular purpose (e.g., to find something out, to see what happens, to check if something happens), students may remember different details or none at all.

Similarly, if you give the same current events article to teachers across all the departments in your middle or high school, the science teachers will pay attention to different details than the history teachers, who will pay attention to different details than the math teachers. If we don't set a purpose for reading, people read with their own individual lenses and keep track of what is most interesting to them. If students are lucky, it matches what their teachers were interested in and they do well on tests and tasks related to that reading. If they're unlucky, they read the text with comprehension, but may deprioritize some of the details that they could lose points for not knowing. Readers have a right to know why they are reading what they are reading in school contexts so that they can use text successfully in class.

Sometimes teachers assume students have a purpose for reading because it is implied by the lesson or unit. However, when a purpose is explicitly (re)stated before reading, students read and understand more with less support. For example, I asked a group of high school teachers representing different content areas to use this fill-in-the-blank sentence at least once over a two-week period and report back about what happened:

Today we are going to read _____ by _____ -ing in order to _____.

The sentence frame ensures students have a purpose (*in order to*) and process (*by*) for reading before they begin. To my surprise and delight, when I asked the sixteen teachers to share what they found, not only had all sixteen tried it, but nearly all sixteen had used it three or more times because they were so happy with what they saw. Observations ranged from students getting started more efficiently and finishing the reading without prompting, to understanding texts better on their own and asking better questions when they were finished reading. In one class where students often asked, "What are we doing again?" five, ten, and twenty-five minutes into an activity, the teacher reported no such questions and a decrease in requests for the hall pass. Setting a purpose for reading fuels motivation and success.

In observation Lessons where students read accurately with a purpose can be identified based on these criteria:

1. You should be able to identify clear purposes for reading by:
    a. examining the board or recent posters and anchor charts to see if there is a visual reminder of a goal or reason for reading
    b. asking students, "Why are you reading what you're reading?" or "What made you choose this text?"
    c. asking students what they will do as a result of their reading when they have finished it: "What will you be able to do/say/have when you have read this text?"

A clearly stated purpose for reading develops *value* and *intrinsic* reasons for motivation and engagement. Some students may need some prompting if their primary reason for reading was to comply with directions. However, if students cannot come up with a reason for reading a particular text on a particular day, it is unlikely that they have a sense of the task's *value* to fuel their motivation and engagement.

2. You should find evidence that students had the opportunity to read accurately by:
    a. noticing that more than one text was available for students to read during some part of the lesson either because students were given several options, a set of texts, or a choice of what to read

    b. noticing that students have opportunities to engage with the same text in more- and less-supported environments (whole group, small group, independently)

    c. noticing that students had the opportunity to read and reread a text that was read aloud if it was particularly challenging: repeated reading of a challenging text, when supported by a model, indicates an investment in developing accuracy despite text complexity.

These demonstrate the possibility of *most* students having an opportunity to read accurately. This develops knowledge and *self-efficacy* simultaneously. If everyone is always reading the same text in the same way, you can guarantee the majority of students are not engaging in optimal practice even if they are compliant.

Writing with a purpose and audience

There have been a series of great debates that run through the history of writing instruction. Should there be explicit grammar instruction? Should paragraphs and essays be free-form or formulaic? Can writing be graded objectively? Can good writing be taught?

Writing (like reading) is, at its core, a purpose-driven activity. It uses visual representations for connection between people and ideas across time and space. All of its rules, structures, and conventions are derived from the human imperative to communicate. Too often, however, writing is taught as either mechanical or mystical: as a set of rules to be learned, or an art form that only a few people are born to practice well.

If we want students to become flexible, powerful writers, we cannot teach writing in a way that is divorced from purpose, audience, or creativity. Similarly, we cannot teach writing without making the tools, conventions, and norms of communication explicit to students as we go. Though writing instruction can take many forms, the hallmarks of powerful writing activities are a clear purpose and audience, which become the target and rationale for learning about conventions like grammar and punctuation, or genre-level features like sentence, paragraph, or essay structures and devices.

After synthesizing research on writing and the connection between the reading and writing, in some of the most-cited reports in literary history (see Graham and Hebert 2010), Graham and Harris (2016) published a list of eight evidence-based practices for writing instruction in *The Reading Teacher*. The first one is: Write.

Write. Yes. But, how? Summarizing a set of surveys from students and classroom teachers conducted periodically over the last several decades, Applebee and Langer (2009) noted, "What is clear is that even with some increases over time, many students are not writing a great deal for any of their academic subjects, including English, and most are not writing at any length" (18). More recent surveys of middle and high school teachers confirm that teachers and schools have yet to incorporate writing into the curriculum in systematic ways (Applebee and Langer 2011, 2009; Graham et al. 2014).

Still there is a long and rich history of research to support evidence-based writing instruction. The list in Figure 4.2 from Graham and Harris (2016) could be used as a starting point for discussions about writing instruction, but more importantly, it offers support for the idea that purpose and audience matter.

What unites each of the evidence-based practices is the sensitivity to the weight of the task of composition: it requires practice, purposes, comfort, direction, explanation, knowledge of process, and specialized tools. These features are interconnected so that if you invest in one, it supports the others like spokes on a wheel with purpose, audience, and format at the center.

As Graham and Hebert (2010) have shown, the most successful writing instruction balances explicit instruction on grammar and mechanics, with explicit instruction about the process of writing with genre-specific features. A well-formed sentence in the midst of a poorly organized piece with an incoherent voice and a mishmash of genre features will not be well understood by any audience. And a well-organized piece with sentence-level errors of spelling and punctuation is not only difficult to understand, but likely to be misunderstood.

By the same token, if writing instruction focuses only on the nitty-gritty details of convention and form, students will not know how to communicate with an audience for a purpose.

Much of the writing students do throughout the school day is not in the context of formal writing instruction (Applebee and Langer 2009). Especially in content area classes, students are most often writing down notes, answers to questions, and short demonstrations of knowledge. These informal writing tasks may not address Common Core State Standards language or literature objectives, because they are aimed at teaching/learning discipline-specific knowledge. In these cases, it is even more important for students to have a purpose, audience, and format in mind, so that the very form and function of their discipline-specific writing reflects the nature of that discipline.

6 Evidence-Based Practices for Writing Instruction

	Evidence	Questions for Discussion
1. Write	• Students in classrooms that write more average a 12 percentage point gain in writing quality and a 14 percentage point lead on measures of reading comprehension compared to students who write for less time on average.	• When students write each day: Who are they writing to? For what reason are they writing?
2. Write to comprehend and learn	• Students who write about what they are reading jump 24 percentile points on measures of text comprehension. • Students who write about content they learned in class jump 9 percentile points on content knowledge.	• At what stage(s) of a lesson do students write most often? Where else could short, informal writing be used?
3. Create a pleasant and motivating writing environment	• Exemplary writing teachers encourage self-regulation, positive messages about effort and high, realistic expectations. • Feedback on what and how students are writing is associated with a 16 percentage point jump in writing quality.	• How would students know they are writing well? How do students know the impact of their writing? • Is student writing visible in the room or school building?
4. Facilitate students' writing as they compose	• A clear, specific goal for writing is associated with a 28 percentile point jump in writing quality. • Students who plan, edit, and revise with their peers demonstrate a 31 percentage point gain in writing quality.	• How do you set clear goals for each pocket of time spent writing? • What resources can students use to support their writing during these sessions?
5. Teach critical skills, processes, and knowledge	• Gathering and organizing ideas before writing is associated with a 21 percentile point jump in writing quality. • Teaching sentence construction and combination is associated with a 21 percentile point jump in writing quality because students can then compose grammatically correct sentences automatically. • Teaching attributes of specific types of writing and conventions of specific genres is associated with a 21 percentile point jump in writing quality.	• When you co-construct text with students, what is easiest/hardest for them to contribute? What do you do as a writer that you have yet to see your students do?
6. Use twenty-first-century writing tools	• Writing on a computer or tablet allows students to create publishable drafts of their work. • Writing online increases the audiences, purposes and formats to which students have access as writers.	• What formats and genres might be available if some assignments are completed online? • What audiences might be reached if students published their work digitally?

FIGURE **4.2** Graham and Harris' Six Evidence-Based Practices with Related Questions (2016)

It is also important for them to see and discuss good examples of writing—both formal and informal—so that these examples can serve as mentors that can be copied and critiqued to provide support and understanding of how written texts work. Writing assignments, even brief exit slips, that include an intentional match between purpose, audience, and format can contribute to both content and literacy learning simultaneously (Gabriel, Wenz, and Dostal 2016)—especially when students have the opportunity to write after viewing and discussing model/mentor texts. (See Figure 4.3.)

In observation Writing with a purpose to an audience can be identified based on these criteria:

1. Both teachers and students reference a specific person or group (audience) when making decisions about what to write and how to represent ideas using words, sentences, and punctuation. Students should be able to fill in these blanks: I/we are writing to _____ because/in order to _____.
2. The format of the writing task matches the stated purpose and audience every time, whether students are writing to demonstrate what they know about content or writing in the context of a lesson focused on the writing process.
3. There is a balance between language and literature objectives within and across lessons to be sure students have both the *what* and the

FIGURE **4.3**
Purpose Audience
Format Triangle

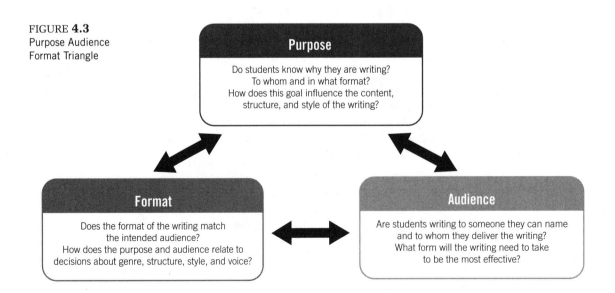

Purpose

Do students know why they are writing?
To whom and in what format?
How does this goal influence the content,
structure, and style of the writing?

Format

Does the format of the writing match
the intended audience?
How does the purpose and audience relate to
decisions about genre, structure, style, and voice?

Audience

Are students writing to someone they can name
and to whom they deliver the writing?
What form will the writing need to take
to be the most effective?

why of composition. If you see teachers addressing only one or the other, you might ask about when this will be balanced out in upcoming lessons.

Talking about text with teachers and peers

Classroom discourse is a feature of every commercially available observation rubric. Though each rubric specifies features of talk—like questioning, discussion, and participation patterns—in different ways, there is profound agreement that classroom talk is a marker of classroom quality. According to comparisons between observation tools in the Measures of Effective Teaching (MET) project, measures of classroom discourse are among the most predictive of all other measures of teaching quality, including student achievement and teacher effect scores (MET Project 2012; Hill and Grossman 2016).

The reason talk is so important for learning, specifically literacy learning, is that it involves and provides occasion for the kind of cognitive processing required for learning in an efficient and observable way. Reading a text, watching a movie, or listening to a teacher are all forms of gathering—as if ideas, tools, and processes are being activated and loaded into a blender.

The result of this largely passive gathering is not immediate learning or proficiency: learning requires some sort of active processing of this new information, practice with new tools, or application of a new skill.

Saying something in your own words and discussing or asking/answering questions about it all require that students select and organize language to communicate about this new raw material they have gathered. Talking is pressing "blend." Students are, in effect, using language to learn language.

A few other activities can also press blend in different ways—writing, drawing, or acting things out—essentially taking raw information and expressing it in a different way than it was received. The important thing about talk in particular is that it is a social medium; it directly involves or encourages social interactions (unlike journaling or drawing), thus students have social support for learning as well as the benefit of the dynamic, diverse approximations of their peers to shape and refine their emerging understandings.

Classrooms where students are talking about text are classrooms where students are learning about text. In observation, evaluators can differentiate talk about text from "just talk" by listening for mention of the text, the act of reading, or the content of the text. What sounds like social talk about characters, chapters, authors, and so on may very well be an example of literate practice: the social discussion of the printed word. Sentence stems and formal discussion or debate do not mark the presence of literate talk as much as the mention of texts and their authors.

The goal for literacy classroom discourse is to apprentice students into the practice of textual chitchat. This is why Harvey Daniels describes literature circles as similar to adult book clubs without the wine: the purpose of learning to be literate is to have social discussions about texts, authors, contexts, content, and the process of being a reader with others—to connect with others around the printed word. Of course many adults do not join these kinds of book clubs, but still read for work, pleasure, and a combination of the two. Even without the social scene of book clubs, reading is very often a social activity: we read and write to be able to talk to one another about what we've read or do something together as a result of what we've read. Very often, our colleagues, peers, friends, and family are each other's reasons for reading.

In observation Talking about text with teachers and peers can be identified based on these criteria:

1. Students have the opportunity to engage in back-and-forth discussions with the teacher (in a conference) or with peers (in small- or whole-group settings) that focus on something they wrote or read.
2. When students are talking in class, they are talking about texts they are preparing to read/write or in the process of reading/writing.
3. Teachers and students can name examples of discussions they have had, either individually or in groups, about the texts they are reading or writing this week. Evaluators that see reading/writing in progress might ask, "Have you gotten to talk to someone about this piece yet? Do you think you will?"

Discussing models of fluent reading and expert writing

Language is naturally and implicitly acquired, but literacy isn't. We need to welcome students into the reading and writing club not only by exposing them to text and purposes for reading and writing but by showing them exactly *how* we read and write. More specifically, students need to be able to identify the processes readers use to make meaning and send messages using text to internalize these processes for use on their own.

Notice that it is not just "models of expert reading and writing" that count as an active ingredient. Mere exposure may be supportive of some students, but a discussion of what is being modeled, how the work of reading and writing is being accomplished, is supportive of many more. Studies of teacher think-alouds with discussion of how and why the teacher is doing what he's doing consistently demonstrate better transfer of practices from teacher to student.

Naming, showing, and discussing skills and strategies in action is what translators say Lev Vygotsky (1978) described as the necessary "defossilization" of complex practices: the cognitive disassembly of what experts experience as automatic or fluid motion. Instead of showing a snapshot of reading in progress, teachers show it step by step, as if in slow motion, with language and discussion attached to each step. This approach to making thinking visible, or externalizing thinking, shows the hidden magic behind skilled practice and exposes the process to students who can then attempt each step while being coached or assisted with the process as a whole. It also requires that teachers know what they are doing when they read/write so that they can explain to students how and why they have strategically, if unconsciously, modified their process to accomplish certain things.

The need to not only narrate but discuss literate process as it occurs is familiar within learning-by-doing approaches and apprenticeship models. The focus of instructional language is on the *process*, of doing skilled tasks, not on the product. For example, you would not hear hockey coaches teaching players to take slap shots by telling them "watch and then try," over and over again. You see them slow the swing down into slow motion, narrating what they're doing as they go in a series of steps that each has a purpose: line up the puck with your inside foot, reach back while your lower hand slides down, twist from your hip, connect with the ice an inch before the puck, lift and snap your wrist while your weight comes forward. That's a mouthful to say all at once, so it takes a few models, with a few different narrations and observations from different angles. Once students know the process and have language to discuss its parts, a coach can truly coach: "Almost there, but next time slide your left hand lower." "Didn't work because you forgot to line up the puck." "Yes, but snap your wrist harder." They can identify the part of the instantaneous, automatic process that needs fixing or finesse in a way that promotes the conscious acquisition of complex skills.

Of course, some players, like some readers, get lucky or pick things up faster than others, or seem to naturally do efficient, effective things without being told. But, at some point we all need language attached to defossilized practice in order to reanimate it and appropriate it as our own.

In observation Discussing models of fluent reading and expert writing can be identified based on these criteria:

1. Teachers name and narrate what they are doing and why as they engage in reading or writing in front of students (model). They may leave a visual reminder of the processes they demonstrate, as steps, directions, reminders, or anchor charts to which students may refer. However, these charts cannot exist in isolation: their contents also require live demonstration and opportunities for student practice.

2. Descriptions of all steps of the writing process and exemplars of informal writing are outlined on anchor charts or other visual reminders. These are then demonstrated by teachers and practiced by students.

3. Students can describe or reference lists of criteria for success as readers and writers (e.g., what expert readers do, what expert writers do, what "we" are working toward).

Interventions that support individuals and focus on meaning

Interventions, by definition, are meant to *alter the course of events*. That is, reading interventions must either correct the course of development by addressing misconceptions or inefficient habits or alter the trajectory of development by dramatically increasing the rate of change. We can increase the rate of change by making interventions more *intensive* and more *expert* than regular instruction in either subtle or profound ways. But, when interventions are neither more expert nor more intensive, they are more than just a waste of time: they may cause cycles of reading failure by reinforcing confusion, frustration, or inefficient/ineffective reading habits.

Intensive There are two major strategies for making intervention instruction more intensive than regular classroom instruction. The lightest is simply allocating more time for more practice or exposure. This strategy assumes students are on the right track, have developed the appropriate skills and strategies, but simply need more opportunities to apply what they know to solidify and extend it. This gift of time, however, is only helpful if the student does not require additional support or targeted instruction and feedback.

One way to increase the intensity of extra time is to limit the student-teacher ratio, so that students have greater access to individualized explanations, coaching, and feedback. A smaller group size also allows teachers to individualize the focus of the intervention so that students receive instruction in the areas they need support, rather than in all areas at once. A family of studies conducted over the last fifteen years have consistently confirmed that there are several predictable profiles of struggling readers, each of which requires a different instructional focus (Spear-Swerling 2014; Dennis 2012; Leseaux and Kieffer 2010; Valencia 2010). In other words, struggling readers are not a homogeneous group that will all benefit from the same intervention (Figure 4.4). If interventions are the same for all readers who struggle, some will inevitably waste time working on areas of relative strength and not receive intensive instruction in the areas of relative weakness.

FIGURE **4.4**
Studies That Identify Profiles of Struggling Readers

Profiles of Struggling Readers			
	Word ID	Meaning	Fluency
Valencia and Riddle-Buly (2002); Valencia (2010): 108 fifth graders			
Automatic word callers	++	–	++
Struggling word callers	–	–	++
Word stumblers	–	+	–
Slow comprehenders	+	++	–
Slow word callers	+	–	–
Disabled readers	––	––	––
Dennis (2012): 94 sixth to eighth graders			
Slow and steady comprehenders	+	+	–
Slow word callers	+	–	––
Automatic word callers	+	–	+
Struggling word callers	–	––	+
Rupp and Lesaux (2006): 1,111 fourth graders			
Below expectations with significantly lower word-level skills	––	–/+	––
Below expectations with significantly higher word-level skills	+	–	+
Leach, Scarborough, and Rescorla (2003): 141 fourth graders			
Word-level processing deficits accompanied by adequate comprehension	–	+	–
Weak comprehension skills accompanied by good lower level skills	+	–	+
Both kinds of difficulty	–	–	–

The possibility of greater differentiation and more personalized instruction makes group size a consistent predictor of the power of an intervention. One-to-one instruction is consistently found to be the most powerful, and small groups of 2–5 students are more effective than larger-group or whole-class settings (Hong and Hong 2009; Taylor et al. 1999).

Expert We can make interventions more expert by ensuring students interact with teachers who can do more than just reiterate or simplify classroom instruction. To dramatically change a student's trajectory of development, someone, most often a human, must be able to provide explanations, guidance, or feedback that is *more* specific, clear, or individualized than whatever students receive in their regular classroom. We know "expertise" has been increased if we see the interventionist provide missing background or prerequisite skill practice and provide thoughtful feedback to students as they engage with literate practices in small groups or individually.

Few people would argue that the knowledge base for teaching reading is common knowledge. Yet, there are examples of intervention programs carried out by minimally trained volunteers, paraprofessionals, peers, or close-age mentors that support development simply because the explanations, practice, and feedback are more individualized and therefore more intense (Fitzgerald 2001). However, in general, advanced degrees and certification in reading are good indicators that an educator can provide more and better explanations, coaching, and feedback to students who need it.

A recent meta-analyses of studies examining the efficacy of a range of reading and writing interventions have consistently highlighted four features that separate effective programs from ineffective programs (see Gabriel and Dostal 2015).

1. Effective programs make use of *texts on students' independent level* and/or provide extensive teacher or peer (not computer) support for meaning making with texts at instructional or frustration levels.
   a. Programs that *allow teachers or students to select texts* are consistently more effective than those that prescribe a single program-selected passage for each lesson. The freedom to select texts, even when selecting from a limited set of options, not only supports engagement but allows teachers to personalize text selections for particular students.
2. Effective programs *focus on identifying words and reading fluently* to make meaning. Those that use isolated word lists, nonsense

passages, or disconnected lists of sentences for practice are consistently less effective than those that use meaningful, leveled passages.

3. Effective interventions *involve extensive individual feedback from teachers or peers* that helps students shape and solidify their skills and strategies. Though computer programs can immediately tell students when they are right or wrong, they cannot coach them into correct answers or identify the misconception that underlies their mistakes. Therefore, computerized feedback is therefore generally experienced as frustrating and rarely leads to growth. Conversely, teacher or peer feedback that helps students reshape their processes is associated with significant gains in achievement over time.

4. Interventions that target comprehension include some kind of *discussion*, either oral or in writing, between teachers and students or among students (as with peer-assisted learning). To internalize skills and strategies, even those associated with beginning reading like phonics or phonemic awareness, students need to talk about them. Such talk not only builds metacognition, but may also build background, interest, and knowledge of alternatives that dramatically change students' trajectory of growth.

In addition to the four features listed above, there is no evidence within peer-reviewed research that a computer-delivered intervention can match or exceed the efficacy of a teacher- or tutor-delivered intervention. This is likely because the nature of explanation and quality of feedback within human interactions is key to the success of the intervention. If students merely need more practice and exposure, computer programs may provide an engaging context for this, but should not be considered either more expert or more intensive than regular classroom instruction.

You may also notice that there are parallels between the four features listed above and the active ingredients addressed earlier in the chapter. The difference is merely intensity: where the regular classroom involves discussion between twenty students, an intervention group of two to five students requires four to ten times more interaction, which means up to 400 percent more opportunities for feedback and five times greater likelihood that students will be interacting with a text they can and want to read. Likewise, students struggling with beginning reading skills are more likely to receive explicit modeling and feedback, personalized scaffolds for memory, and practice on exactly the sounds and patterns they need if they are practicing in a small group with an expert instructor.

In observation Interventions that support individuals and focus on meaning could not possibly be the same for every student. Rather, intervention settings should meet the following criteria:

1. Students are grouped according to specific individual needs.
2. Students receive frequent, explicit coaching and feedback from someone who can identify difficulty and address it specifically.
3. Students regularly apply their skills to texts that carry meaning, which are selected by the teacher or student to ensure a good match for optimal practice.
4. Students are invited to discuss what they are doing, why, and how so that they not only perform but internalize the skills and strategies they will need for independent success.

Just as readers learn to identify, analyze, and often emulate elements of author's craft, administrators observing teaching in action often need a nudge to discern where the action is in a literacy lesson (Croninger and Valli 2009). Many of our most powerful teaching moves—like providing a range of interesting and appropriately leveled texts—are indirect, invisible, or asynchronous within a single lesson (Allington 2014). Similarly, many of our most powerful literacy lessons occur in individual one-to-one conversations with or between students, while others are reading quietly in the background. In short, as Nystrand (2006) and others have argued, that which is immediately observable in a literacy lesson may not be what is most important for student growth. Rather, the hallmarks of effective literacy instruction are often in the coordination of activities, the facilitation of opportunities, and the presence of "active ingredients" that prove their value only over time.

A Measure and Sort Approach to Ensuring Effective Literacy Instruction

Because reading, writing, and talking are important, the sort and measure approach to ensuring effective instruction is to mandate a certain number of minutes be spent reading, writing, and talking. This often involves:

- visiting classrooms to ensure appropriate amounts of time are spent on each task
- rewarding teachers who meet or exceed minimum expectations
- creating plans for improving teachers who fail to read, write, and talk enough in class.

A measure and sort approach to effective literacy instruction might also identify "best practices" and create systems that ensure teachers consistently employ those practices in ways that can be monitored and analyzed by supervisors. Compliance with the implementation of these practices would be monitored by school leaders and literacy coaches as evidence of effective teaching. Doing prescribed instruction would be synonymous with doing good teaching. Clearly articulated expectations for teacher behavior, like "teachers call on at least 50 percent of the class to participate in discussions" are easier to enforce than broad statements like "students should be engaged."

Unfortunately, this often overemphasizes the outward appearance of "best practices" while strangling possibilities for personalized, responsive teaching. It is, however, a starting point—and sometimes a necessary starting point, when teachers are transitioning into a new model or out of ineffective practices for the first time.

A Support and Develop Approach to Ensuring Effective Literacy Instruction

Where a sort and measure approach might count turns per student to measure the quality of student discussions, a support and develop approach would keep track of the nature of student contributions (e.g., asking questions, stating opinions, giving examples), not because some of these contributions are better than others but to see what sorts of contributions students are able to make as readers/writers, and whether this repertoire could be extended. In other words, the goal is not to evaluate, but to find possibilities for extending what is going well. When we take a support and develop approach to effective literacy instruction, we're essentially saying, "When it comes to reading improvement, we believe in noticing and extending what individuals do to help them do it more, better, or more efficiently."

Everything from the focus of professional development resources to the focus of instruction itself is aimed at ensuring students (and their teachers) have wide repertoires of skills and strategies to help them accomplish their goals as readers and writers. Instead of measuring the number of behaviors associated with growth (e.g., counting minutes spent reading), evaluators may analyze how individual student needs are/are not being met by the organization of instruction.

This means that each teacher may get different feedback or guidance than their colleagues, or even different feedback for different class periods, based on the needs of the students in their room at the time. There would be few schoolwide mandates about class time, materials, or configurations. Rather, each teacher would be coached to make decisions based on the students they engage with in each class period. The investment here is in teacher thinking rather than teacher behavior. One teacher might be trying more group work with F period and more independent practice with G period. Similarly, though the fourth-grade team members might be focused on persuasive writing, their goal is not to teach it the same way, but to let common principles and shared ideas guide the decisions they make in response to their students.

In a support and develop approach, we assume that what counts as "best" practice varies from classroom to classroom and year to year. This variation by design makes it difficult to sort or measure quality. However, the active ingredients can serve as a litmus test that ensures this flexible approach doesn't just let anything go. If teachers can explain how they are working to optimize opportunities for reading, writing, and talking in their classrooms, evaluators can coach them into strategies that might accomplish these goals given particular students and contexts.

Key Points

- Effective literacy instruction is built using five main active ingredients that you should expect to observe in action for every student, every day:

  » reading accurately with a purpose

  » writing with a purpose and audience

  » talking about text with teachers and peers

  » discussing models of fluent reading and expert writing

  » interventions that support individuals and focus on meaning.

- That which is immediately observable in a literacy lesson may not be what is most important for student growth. Rather, the hallmarks of effective literacy instruction are often in the coordination of activities, the facilitation of opportunities, and the presence of "active ingredients" for literacy learning that prove their value only over time.

Tools to Share

The following tools for Chapter 4 can be found in the appendixes:

- Pocket Version of the "Look-Fors" for Key Ingredients of Effective Literacy Instruction
- Accountability First and Just Read Case Study
- Create Your Own Case Study

Observations of Literacy Instruction

> ▶ *How do tools for evaluation set and limit what counts as effective instruction?*
>
> ▶ *What questions should be asked about the critical aspects of instruction that cannot be seen?*

One spring, as part of a professional development series on the workshop model of literacy instruction, I (Rachael) modeled a writing minilesson that had an embedded assessment for a group of third- to fifth-grade teachers from the same district. I wrote and rewrote the lesson, I rehearsed it aloud for my dogs, I even (sheepishly) ran it by a colleague who studies writing instruction to make sure what I was showing them was worth seeing.

The benefit of modeling lessons for a group of teachers at a professional development day is that I learn what they think their evaluators are looking for—because that's what they demand from me. So, fueled by the adrenaline of running in almost late for my own workshop, I pulled it off without a hitch. Then I opened the floor for discussion.

An experienced teacher called out, "That was more than twelve minutes. Much more." Her confident and critical tone let me know that she was certain of her feedback. And before I could gather a response, the chatter in the room started.

All the teachers had been told that their minilessons should last ten to twelve minutes. No more, no less. Some had been "dinged" for short lessons, others for long lessons, and some had been dinged in both directions. Thus, many of these teachers had become vigilant about monitoring the length of minilessons instead of the quality of the lesson itself.

It turns out that evaluators in this setting knew that workshop-style lessons were characterized by short minilessons and long independent practice. They also were aware their teachers often held the floor for much more than half the instructional period, leaving very little time or space for independent practice and enabling disorganized—and frequently scattered—teacher-centered instruction. So, they set a time limit on minilessons, reasoning that procedural compliance with the formal structure of a workshop-style lesson would be a first step toward better fidelity to the model. Faithfully following the model, as program developers often remind us, should lead to positive outcomes.

In fact, when teachers are just learning a new approach, following its intended structure allows them to use that structure as a scaffold for their own learning (Valencia et al. 2006), letting them lean on the method and pay attention to their students, instead of their own actions. Following a specific model allows teachers to make fewer decisions about what to do and concentrate more on how to do it.

But, you can have a short, weak minilesson just as easily as a long, powerful minilesson—especially if you only ever receive feedback on the length, rather than the content or delivery of that lesson. For example, a teacher could lead a ten-minute reading comprehension minilesson without clear objectives that engages few students. This lesson is unlikely to benefit students or support a workshop's goal to inspire a love of reading. And, another teacher could teach an innovative writing minilesson that draws on students' background knowledge and that just so happens to take seventeen minutes to complete. In this case, the additional time may enable the teacher to check students' understanding and motivate them to do high-quality independent work.

Two of the fifteen teachers in my workshop were able to use feedback about the timing of their minilessons, and they shortened their lessons as a result. The rest of the group seemed to have learned that (a) they were under timed surveillance when being observed, and (b) this surveillance had to do with instrumental compliance instead of principled practice. As long as their lessons came in no less than ten and no more than twelve minutes, they were doing a good job. They took this as evidence that administrators didn't know much about teaching reading and used it as a reason to discount further feedback. Throughout our workshop they traded war stories of ridiculous feedback conversations (especially feedback that came, unpunctuated, over email) to illustrate this point and generated a general shared distrust of administrative support.

Here's where the administrators are absolutely right: minilessons should be mini. In fact, they should be lean. Concentrated. Specific. Bite-size. They *are* the explicit part of a lesson that involves mostly practice and exposure, so they need to be solid gold, no fluff. They do not, however, need to be exactly twelve minutes.

Here's where the teachers are right: a focus on procedure rather than principle when observing classroom practice has and will always fail to improve instruction. A focus on procedure will lead to teachers making quick adjustments instead of deeper shifts in values and practices. A focus on procedures has too often led both evaluators and researchers to see the forest for some very unhelpful trees, and therefore miss the action in teaching and learning interactions.

Imperfect Tools for Classroom Observation

Current evaluation systems use an assortment of tools to focus classroom observations and score teacher practice. Rubrics and checklists are both the best and worst thing to happen to classroom observations. We love them because they set guidelines, giving observers something to look for and a common language to discuss teaching with teachers. They also encourage observers to look for similar things across classrooms, which helps them make connections and ensures teachers are held to similar standards.

We struggle with them because they both set and limit what counts as effectiveness in teaching. It turns out that observable practices may be easy to evaluate (you know it when you see it), but hard to value (you may not know what it means).

Understanding connections between instruction and achievement

Looking for features of effective instruction, *even when you know what to look for*, is not enough. Too often, it is not the fact that a practice was used that matters, but how it was used, in coordination with other practices, at a particular time, in a particular setting. Moreover, focusing on specific, observable practices may lead to symbolic performances of effective instructional techniques or methods that are surface-level rather than transformational. Decades of research on the link between classroom practices and student achievement have demonstrated this over and over again: what we see upon observation is only weakly related to the outcomes of instruction. We outline just a few highlights from such research below.

Process-product research Between the 1960s and 1980s, a few educational researchers focused on determining the connection between observable teacher and student behaviors (process) and student outcomes (product). Researchers specify an observable behavior to investigate, like praise, and see if there was a correlation between average student achievement in classrooms with more or less instances of praise. However, even if process-product research uncovered *that* a practice was effective, it could not explain *how* or *why* that practice was effective in a particular context. And when practices identified by process-product research were replicated in new settings, they often failed to produce the same outcomes. This is why several decades of well-funded process-product research came under attack (see Gage and Needles 1989). It seems that what you see doesn't guarantee what you'll get when it comes to classroom observation.

Teacher × student interactions Since 2004, researcher Carol Connor and her colleagues have been investigating the idea that a teacher's effect on student achievement actually depends in part on the student. They have developed a multidimensional observation tool, the Individualizing Student Instruction observational protocol, to track how individual students interact with instruction in a given classroom. They have found that "children who share the same classroom have very different learning opportunities, that instruction occurs through interactions among teachers and students, and that the effect of this instruction depends on children's language and literacy skills" (Connor et al. 2009, 85). They conclude, "This means that what is effective for one child may be ineffective for another with different skills." By observing the learning opportunities of a handful of focal students, rather than focusing observations on either teacher behaviors or student behaviors, they have uncovered significant teacher-student interactions and student-environment interactions that explain student outcomes better than simpler, more holistic measures. This blows the idea of a set of singular "best practices" out of the water. For example, they explain:

> A seemingly chaotic classroom where children are working on many child- and peer-managed projects and are expected to manage their own learning (a variety of child-managed learning opportunities) might be a highly stimulating and effective learning environment for a student who brings stronger language and behavioral regulation skills to the classroom. At the same time, our research suggests that such an environment would not provide an effective learning environment for a student with weaker language and behavioral regulation skills. (95)

What looks like chaos may work for some kids, but is unlikely to work for all. By the same token, what looks like quiet order may work for some kids, but is unlikely to work for all. The goal, Connor and colleagues argue, is to intentionally plan instruction to attend to the individual differences in the room. In other words, to differentiate learning experiences for students, so that students' inevitable individual differences do not differentiate for you. Instruction that is more diagnostic, responsive, and dynamic is more likely to produce positive outcomes than instruction that exemplifies a pre-selected set of best practices.

The non-negotiables checklist As part of our study of the Measures of Effective Teaching Project Longitudinal Database, we developed a checklist that focused on five non-negotiable, active ingredients of literacy instruction. Following Dr. Atul Gawande's logic in the best-selling *Checklist Manifesto*, we reasoned that if we were to give evaluators a simple, commonsense framework for evaluating literacy instruction, we might accurately identify classrooms in need of immediate intervention. So, we watched more than 200 videos of fourth- and eighth-grade reading lessons and asked ourselves this simple set of questions at two-minute intervals:

Are they reading, writing, or talking about text? If so, how?

We rated teachers based on the percent of classroom time they dedicated to either reading, writing, or talking. We added bonus points if instruction included mention of reading strategies, modeling, or differentiated texts or tasks. We then compared our ratings to ratings from three popular rubrics and teachers' value-added scores (based on student test scores). We found very little relationship between our ratings and others. Our hunch was that it matters more *how and why* students are reading, writing, and talking than *whether* they spend a certain number of minutes doing so. It matters more how teachers manage twenty minutes of writing than the fact that they schedule twenty minutes of writing. Similarly, talk about text that involves the four most talkative students instead of all the students—including those not inclined to talk—is a more powerful indicator than the fact that a class discussion took place. In other words: looking for specific indicators doesn't guarantee we know quality when we see it. We need to ask how each non-negotiable element is enacted, not just check off that it was there.

So, we took a closer look at very high-scoring teachers (top 1 percent) and very low-scoring teachers (bottom 1 percent). We found evidence of the non-negotiables in both sets of classrooms. However, we noticed some sharp differences in *how* these non-negotiables were enacted. For example, both high- and low-scoring fourth-grade classrooms included teacher read-alouds. But in low-scoring classrooms the teacher interrupted the read-aloud to comment, ask a lower-order question (e.g., what just happened?), or manage behavior every minute or two. In higher-scoring classrooms, the teacher read continuously for several minutes at a time and only stopped to wonder something aloud, or ask questions, at stopping places that made sense within the text (e.g., end of a section or chapter). This means that students were not only exposed to the words in a read-aloud, but they are exposed to cohesive sections of text with few interruptions.

Another example was the length of texts read and written. Lower-scoring classrooms all had students read and write *some*thing. But often it was a sentence or less at a time (e.g., worksheet or grammar drill) rather than the more continuous text of a paragraph, passage, or chapter (for reading), or a response in complete sentences rather than a fill-in response (for writing). The longer and more purposeful the literate activity, the more likely teachers and students were to score well on a range of measures.

Likewise, both lower- and higher-scoring classrooms included some review of lessons or topics that had already been taught. But higher-scoring classrooms used review as a warm-up that built toward a new or continuing lesson while lower-scoring classrooms spent the entire period "reviewing" something that had been taught either because it was never mastered or as preparation for an upcoming test.

Interestingly, 100 percent of the classrooms in which teachers were addressing behavior rather than teaching for sixty seconds or more out of a thirty-minute observation were low-scoring classrooms. We do not believe this is because good management is necessarily a prerequisite for good instruction. Rather, we believe the focus, purpose, and intention evident in high-scoring classrooms leaves less room or reason for misbehavior. If students are exposed to coherent stories and engaged with continuous texts, and if they approach something new each day (rather than reviewing or engaging with fragments of text for a whole period), there were fewer incidences of misbehavior. It seems to us that good management and good teaching are not merely codependent, but inseparable.

Weak links between standards-based instruction and student achievement
Most recently, educational researchers determined that the alignment of instruction with standards is only weakly related to the effectiveness of teachers based on student test scores (Polikoff and Porter 2014). Polikoff

and Porter's 2014 study using the same MET Project database examined whether lessons that were more aligned or less aligned to state standards were associated with higher test scores and teacher evaluation ratings. They reluctantly concluded that teachers whose instruction better aligned to the standards often got lower ratings than teachers who ignored standards. And attention to standards did not seem to be strongly linked with student achievement scores either. So, simply asking *whether* teachers address certain standards and objectives in their lessons is not as important as asking *how* they manage to do so.

Inherent bias in observation tools Finally, researchers have just begun to scratch the surface of questions about the potential for inherent bias within the structure and content of commercially available rubrics for the evaluation of teacher or classroom quality. One pioneer of this line of inquiry, Francesca Lopez, who investigated the Classroom Assessment Scoring System (CLASS; LaParo, Pianta, and Hamre 2008), which is often used to assess the quality of HeadStart programs and has been used in several large-scale research studies, including the MET project. Lopez (2011) found that CLASS ratings accurately predicted students' achievement in classrooms where students were *predominantly* non-Hispanic, but the same teacher behaviors did not accurately predict student achievement in classrooms with predominantly Hispanic students.

This is likely because the instrument was validated on a sample of ethnically homogeneous students. That is, when researchers tested whether CLASS predicted student achievement, they did so using classrooms and test scores of predominantly white, monolingual students. Therefore, the tool is likely to be most valid for white, monolingual students. This may be true for other rigorously validated tools as well, but relatively few studies have investigated the potential bias of empirically validated tools thus far. More research has attended to the possibility of observer bias, which can never be fully eliminated, without questioning the bias inherent in the tools themselves. For example, studies in four districts found that teachers whose students have higher incoming achievement levels routinely receive classroom observation scores that are higher on average than those received by teachers whose incoming students score at lower levels (Lindquist, Whitehurst, and Chingos 2014).

Such bias is not a reason to distrust or discount such tools, but it is a reason to use them with discretion and healthy skepticism if you are applying them in contexts other than those within which they were developed.

In light of the long history of studies that demonstrate we do not "know it when we see it" and that "seeing is not enough," here are some principles of observation that connect to student achievement:

Principles of Observation That Connect to Student Achievement

1. You can't look for everything at the same time; you have to know what to look for. This is why rubrics and checklists can come in handy: as focusing tools that support shared language and expectations.

2. You have to know who you're looking at (teacher × student interactions): some practices support some students more than others, so you need to know who is in the room and how the teacher has coordinated practices to support diverse students (Connors et al. 2009; Gabriel and Rojas 2015).

3. You have to be aware of the range of influences on teacher decision making (instructional guidance materials, recent professional development, available resources). Observed practices may be more of an expression of what the teacher feels constrained or required to do than what she would and could do if given the resources and permission. This is why the observation process has to be a two-way street in which the evaluator asks questions to learn more about a teacher's rationale for doing A instead of C.

Is quality really in the eye of the beholder?

On the same day that I was observing a middle school classroom for a research project, the vice principal happened to be in that classroom conducting a walk-through observation. The district guidance for walk-throughs involved picking one row of the rubric at a time as a focus for evaluation, and this month it was the row related to the structure and quality of student participation. During this lesson, the teacher spent forty of her fifty-three minutes going over a set of five sentence corrections from their Daily Oral Language program. During this time she had called on all the students, mostly equitably. Many had the opportunity to go up to the board to correct a sentence. All students were well behaved or very quietly off-task until called on. The lesson was scored as a roaring success: exemplary marks for participation, student engagement, and student discourse.

Without the lens of these rubric rows, I viewed this lesson as a total failure. An unfortunate waste of time. The class read a total of five disconnected, nonsensical sentences. They fixed a total of twelve errors. They called out lots of wrong reasons for correcting sentences along with all the right reasons for correcting them, which indicated to me that they were mostly guessing, not naming or applying internalized patterns or rules.

There is nothing wrong with doing sentence corrections or a Daily Oral Language curriculum, but there is something wrong with using 80 percent of time allocated for literacy instruction for something that has very little to do with reading for meaning, fluency, or word recognition.

The administrator left impressed. I, however, left depressed. We were both wrong. I was right that students had few opportunities to develop literacy: very little reading, no writing, and limited discussion about text. The administrator was right that students were engaged and participating in appropriate, equal, and respectful ways.

What we didn't know, because we didn't ask, was that the teacher was gearing up for her first peer editing activity during an upcoming writing lesson. She wanted students to feel confident about their ability to identify word- and sentence-level errors. She also wanted to ensure there was respectful discussion of word choices and sentence structures so that editing kept a friendly and productive tone.

Though Daily Oral Language was part of her daily routine, this was the only day of the year that it lasted more than five minutes. She had a thoughtful and well-reasoned rationale for the lesson her administrator loved and I hated. It made way for a more productive and more equitable upcoming lesson involving peer editing (which *did* have lots of reading, writing, and talking about text). Although I still disagree that this particular lesson should have received a high rating for effectiveness, I don't disagree with the teacher's decision to invest in student confidence, engagement, and discourse patterns in support of the next day's lesson.

Not *whether*, but *how* questions for teacher evaluation

In some high schools, there are days when the instruction observed during walk-throughs consistently misses the mark. On one such day, the day before a vacation, I accompanied a district leader on walk-through observations of each English department classroom during the school's third period of the day. We saw two classrooms showing movies to mostly sleeping teenagers for what seemed to be the entire period (we walked by a few times). We saw two classrooms with notes on their doors saying they had gone to the computer lab to type essays. And we saw one classroom having an informal discussion about a current event from the morning paper that only some the kids had happened to read.

We didn't see evidence that there were objectives for student learning (posted or implied by activities). We didn't observe any students reading or writing (unless typing an already-written essay counts). We saw a discussion in one out of the five classrooms. So, we had three choices for responses at the end of the day. We could respond to this underwhelming sample of instruction by:

1. *Ignoring it.* We could assume the day before vacation isn't a good day to work and we could try walk-throughs again some other time.
2. *Legislating it.* We could make a rule that students have to be reading, writing, or talking for some part of the period, every period, so that a teacher would be breaking a rule and could be held accountable if he chose to show a movie for all fifty-three minutes of instructional time.
3. *Asking about it.* We could ask teachers about their choices, intentions, and goals for using class time the way they did.

This time we chose to ask and it saved us a lot of time. We found, for example, that one movie-showing teacher had planned to connect the movie to an upcoming reading and writing assignment, but needed support to think about how students could be active consumers of the film (stopping to discuss, taking notes, and write responses) in a way that would set them up to succeed on the reading and writing tasks that were coming up. This was a case of a good faith effort to hook students into a reading/writing task using film, without the pedagogical content knowledge to execute the intention effectively. Legislating time spent reading wouldn't have helped this teacher develop another approach, and neither would ignoring it.

The other movie-showing teacher had a firm belief that the day before break is a throwaway day and any attempted lesson would be a failure anyway. This was a case of low expectations for teaching and learning. Assuming that if we came back another day things would be different was likely to waste time and maybe even affirm the teacher's low expectations by failing to address them. Legislating a rule about the number of minutes students have to read/write/talk might lead to instrumental compliance, but teachers who don't believe students can learn are not likely to comply in meaningful ways. In other words, neither of the first two options were likely to challenge or shift the teacher's beliefs and practices. Asking the teacher what she was thinking didn't change her beliefs either, but it did show us that the root of the problem we observed in two similar classrooms was actually quite different, and probably deserved a different response.

We suggested this teacher talk to the first about how a movie might be fine, if it was surrounded by literate practice (reading, writing, talking). You do not have to introduce new material the day before a break, but there is always room to engage in literate practice. If you need to see it to believe it: you can look next door.

Asking how rather than whether questions surfaces a teacher's goals, strategies, and rationales so that they can be stretched, elaborated, or adjusted. In other words, how questions also create opportunities for teachers to articulate and elaborate their professional decision-making.

The benefit of asking the teacher why and how he engaged in the instruction you observed creates a two-way street for teachers to do some telling and explaining instead of only being on the receiving end of the conversation. It creates an opportunity for evaluators to learn from the many educators they evaluate over time. If teachers are unsure about their goals, are missing strategies, or have no clear rationale for their actions, this—rather than the particular practice—is the problem.

A Measure and Sort Approach to Observing Classroom Instruction

New-generation teacher evaluation systems often overstate the value and importance of classroom observations. Observation scores are included for a large percentage of a teacher's overall score because they are the closest, most authentic measure of teacher quality when compared to things like student test scores, surveys, and growth goals. Studies like the MET project have demonstrated that observation ratings can have a relationship to student test scores and other measures of teacher effectiveness, though this relationship is often weak and unreliable. Still, we have to be careful about the claims we can make based on a small sample of instruction and be honest about the possibility that the most important active ingredients for learning are not visible to the naked eye in real time—they may reveal themselves over time, may be hidden in the subtext of interactions, and may be more powerful for some students than others.

A measure and sort approach to observations of literacy learning relies on the weak correlations between observable practices and student achievement to generate numerical data that represent something about classroom instruction. This is better than ignoring classroom instruction when calculating teacher quality, but is always partial and potentially biased both because of the observation tools themselves (e.g., rubrics and checklists) and due to the complex and contingent nature of teaching and learning interactions (see Figure 5.1).

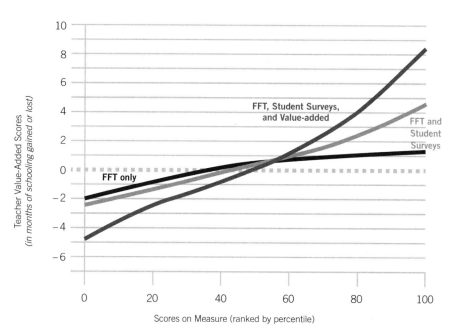

Multiple Measures and Value-Added on State Math Test

FIGURE **5.1**
Multiple Measures and Value-Added on State Math Test from the Measures of Effective Teaching Project

NOTES: Value-added estimated in student-level standard deviation units and converted to months of schooling using a conversion factor of 0.25 standard deviations = 9 months of schooling. Slopes were calculated as running regressions. Teachers' value-added scores and scores of measures were from working with different groups of student. Combined measure was created with equal weights.

A Support and Develop Approach to Observing Classroom Instruction

Returning to the example of the ten- to twelve-minute minilessons at the beginning of this chapter, we might note that time is important in literacy lessons, and a deep and compelling research base has demonstrated the need to invest time in optimal practice, engaged reading, and purposeful writing. Reader's and writer's workshop approaches are grounded, in part, on this very research. A principled expression of that commitment to investing in lean lessons and long practice can't be measured in ticks of the clock, but, instead, should be identified by looking for signs or evidence

FIGURE **5.2**
Principle and Practice
Correlation

of the principle that time spent reading/writing matters (see Figure 5.2). Sometimes principled practice is not observable: it requires asking the teacher why and how she was working toward a certain goal.

Principle: Provide opportunities for students to engage with text				
Practice	Time for independent reading	Shared reading of engaging materials	Individual choice of reading materials	Time to select books in library	Motivation/ incentives for home and summer reading
Rubric representation	Yes	Yes	Yes	Not represented	
Distinguished indicator on the Framework for Teaching	3c: *Instructional materials and resources* are suitable to the instructional goals and engage students mentally. Students initiate the choice, adaptation, or creation of materials to enhance their own purposes.	3c: The lesson's *structure* is highly coherent, allowing for reflection and closure as appropriate. Pacing of the lesson is appropriate for all students.	3c: *Instructional materials and resources* are suitable to the instructional goals and engage students mentally. Student initiate the choice, adaptation, or creation of materials to enhance their own purposes.		

Even and especially when evaluators are not deeply engaged with the theory and principles behind the instruction they observe, they should be most concerned with the how and why of teacher actions. Instead of asking themselves, "Does the teacher talk for X percent of the lesson?," a support and develop approach involves asking, "How is the teacher using her talk within this lesson?"

Instead of asking, "Are the students reading for at least twenty minutes a day?," evaluators might ask, "How does the teacher manage and encourage independent reading?"

- Observations should zoom in on principles rather than practices.
- Teachers and leaders can use rubrics as tools to develop a common language.
- Feedback conversations are a venue for leaders to learn more about teacher practice.

Tools to Share

The following tool for Chapter 5 can be found in the appendixes:

- Surface Features and Underlying Processes

Giving and Getting Effective Feedback

▶ *How can leaders formulate feedback that teachers will receive well and use?*

▶ *How can teachers make something out of unwanted, inaccurate, or otherwise ineffective feedback?*

(Rachael) remember the first time my assistant principal observed me teaching as a first-year teacher in Washington, DC. Four of my five sections of seventh-grade English students had already cycled through our big classroom with its massive windows and dusty chalkboards. I was breathless and nervous when she finally walked in partway through the lesson. I had probably talked to her a hundred times already that year without feeling intimidated, but when she sat down in the back row with her laptop open, she seemed so official—so much more of an adult than I could pretend to be. I think I mostly hid behind my humming, hot overhead projector, only moving to pick up a dropped pen and capture a few student responses on the board behind me.

My assistant principal did not stay long during this observation. When students transitioned to partner work, she stood up from the back row with her laptop and made for the door. On the way out she leaned over to whisper something in my ear. "Nice job, Ms. Gabriel." She said. "By the way, your underwear is showing."

My heart hit the floor. Not so much that a sliver of black was showing above my pants in front of my kids—I had made so many mistakes in front of them and felt so silly and so naked (figuratively) that this seemed insignificant in the grand scheme of things. I was upset that she would think I was sloppy or unprofessional. I was twenty-two and already felt like a fraud most of the time. More than that, I was worried she would think it was a sign of disrespect to the children, the school, the work of teaching

English. I was worried that she would judge this and see nothing else—that the feedback I was anxiously anticipating at our meeting the following week would be about appropriate dress instead of instruction. Still, I was in need of some immediate "technical assistance"—advice about something I could fix on the spot—and she gave it to me. Thank goodness.

As I replayed her words over and over again in my head throughout the day, the first part finally settled in enough to stop my mind from racing with second guesses about what I should have done differently. It started with, "Nice job, Ms. Gabriel." Of course, I convinced myself she was just saying that to be polite—that the real feedback was saved for later. Still, it was enough to help me concentrate beyond my second guesses over the next week as I awaited our thirty-minute debrief meeting. "Nice job." Phew. That's a place to start. And the underwear thing? I'm glad she told me immediately so that I could fix it. The rest of the thirty-minute debrief (I still remember) was about how I chose to explain and apply literary devices as tools for readers. Though I don't remember the specifics of that debrief meeting, I'm not likely to ever forget her message on the way out of the room. Immediate feedback often sticks with people the longest.

There is a special sort of vulnerability that comes with being judged for who you are and what you do based on a fifteen-minute observation, especially when you desperately want to be able to be and do better. And especially if you are new on the job.

At the same time, leaders who care about their teachers may feel like giving feedback is a risk in itself: What if teachers take it the wrong way? What if I'm not right about what I'm telling them? What if they don't know what I mean? It is often easiest to just refrain from giving feedback, especially negative feedback, so that you don't say the wrong thing and ruin the relationship. Leaders are vulnerable in feedback conversations too.

It is important to understand the processes of giving and getting effective feedback because it seems to be the central promise and problem of new-generation evaluation systems. Teachers consistently tell us that they want good feedback and never get enough of it. As the legendary women's basketball coach Pat Summitt said, "In the absence of feedback, people will fill in the blanks with a negative. They will assume you don't care about them or don't like them" (2014, 215). That is why this chapter is all about framing feedback in predictable ways that become second nature to evaluators who want to show their best intentions to teachers in each interaction. It is also about making use of imperfect feedback, because it is likely to be imperfect from time to time, but that doesn't mean there is nothing to learn from it. From the start, we want to acknowledge that the giving and receiving of feedback both take courage, which brings us to another Pat Summitt quote: "A champion is someone who is willing to be uncomfortable" (168).

Teacher evaluation systems are set up to assume that all feedback is helpful feedback. It isn't. Some of it is useless, unmemorable, wrong, offensive, or incomprehensible. Yet, sometimes something as small as a sticky note or as quick as a hallway conversation changes everything. In this chapter, we discuss how the medium can be as important as the message for evaluative feedback, but the messages themselves are still important. If feedback is going to fuel learning it has to be accurate, substantive, and compelling in whatever form it comes. In this chapter on effective feedback, we draw upon three key sources: neuroscience, organizational psychology, and Pat Summit, the winningest coach of all time. Here are some ideas of how to optimize both the giving and receiving of feedback.

Giving Feedback
Feedback as learning fuel

The first thing to keep in mind about feedback is: we are human. We are feeling, thinking beings supported by a biochemistry that responds to feedback in predictable ways. Researchers have demonstrated that your brain can respond to positive feedback the same way it responds to a hug: with the release of the "happiness hormone," oxytocin, which showers your body with warm fuzzy feelings. Negative feedback can stimulate a stress response in which your body produces cortisol, the fight-or-flight stress hormone, which, according to Judith and Richard Glaser (2014) "shuts down the thinking center of our brains and activates conflict aversion and protection behaviors." They explain that this may mean: "We become more reactive and sensitive. We often perceive even greater judgment and negativity than actually exists."

The Glasers have mapped these responses onto certain managerial behaviors and demonstrated how changing communication patterns to include more oxytocin-producing exchanges improves communication and effectiveness of employees in large businesses. Figure 6.1 shows their short list of behaviors managers commonly engage in within conversations with employees, and the hormonal responses they produce.

The bummer is that oxytocin is metabolized comparatively quickly, so its effects do not last as long, whereas cortisol is processed more slowly, even beyond twenty-four hours, so we are more likely to feel the effects for longer. Maybe that is why I remember the feelings of embarrassment and

MANAGERS' POSITIVE AND NEGATIVE CONVERSATIONAL BEHAVIORS
They may be sending mixed messages.

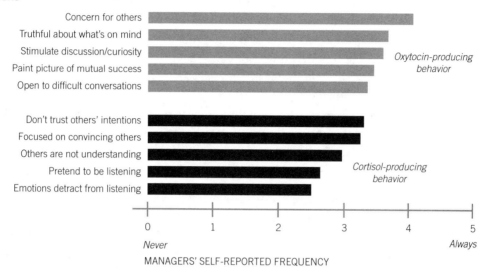

FIGURE **6.1**
Positive and Negative
Supervisor Conversation
Behaviors

disappointment more than whatever constructive or positive comments came with my first observation.

It is important to note, however, that we are not bound by biochemistry or predictable responses to feedback. We may not respect, trust, or even hear certain feedback messages and may therefore respond in unpredictable ways or not at all. Even if you do hear negative messages, and take them to heart, your awareness and understanding of stress can actually change your physical and mental responses to it. Some people orient to stress in ways that are adaptive, productive, and, perhaps counterintuitively, healthy. Psychologists have demonstrated that stress can help provide focus and energy, help people connect or strengthen relationships, and capitalize on the survival instincts of the brain to support learning from stressful stimuli (McGonigal 2015). Psychologist Kelly McGonigal refers to this as "the upside of stress": the ability to harness your natural fight-or-flight response as energized action in a positive direction. I refer to it as "frustration fuel."

If you have ever been told you can't do something and felt challenged, inspired, and energized to do it anyway, you have experienced frustration fuel. You are not bound to feel terrible about bad feedback; you can use it for positive purposes. According to McGonigal, you can:

- Interpret stress responses (like increased heart rate) as *helpful energy* to face a situation, rather than an unpleasant indicator of anger that needs to be quelled or released. This may mean you are more likely to take action as a result of the stress response rather than cope by withdrawing or covering it up.
- View yourself as able to handle and learn from stress so that the feeling of stress does not cause even more stress in a vicious cycle. Instead, you might just notice, rather than stress out about, the feeling of stress.
- View stress as something that is normal for everyone. It can feel terrible, physically and mentally, when you get negative feedback—and knowing that *you are not alone*, this feeling is not forever, and that you are not uniquely flawed to be feeling this way, can help.

Planning for how someone might receive feedback is different from avoiding or sugar-coating it. It means thinking about the context (who else is listening?), specificity (more specific feedback is less likely to feel personal or be devastating), the timing (it should be immediate), and the plan for how this feedback could be addressed. Effective leaders do not rain down good or bad news and run. They focus on moving forward from, rather than just naming, whatever they observed.

Four actions for effective feedback

1. *Honestly sandwiching* the negative inside the positive has long been considered a best practice for feedback across education and other settings, but only if both the positive and negative are actually sincere. Positives can be learning fuel by increasing the confidence and intention teachers bring to their best work. However, teachers, like students, can spot insincerity a mile away. If you can't find anything positive to say, it's likely you have not fully analyzed what you've observed. This is not because there is always necessarily *some*thing good going on, but because the best feedback, like the best teaching, meets the receiver exactly where he is: notices what he is after and what he is "using, but confusing," and sees where his good intentions might have gone wrong.

   For example, I once supervised a student teacher, Vince, who was so focused on student engagement that he turned everything into a game. It was a gift, really, and students who were once apathetic were excited to attend and engage in math class. They high-fived him on the way in and out of class and smiled straight through. However, to make math into games like *Jeopardy!*, 21 Questions, and Trivial Pursuit, Vince was sticking to low-level questions and was more often in review than instruction mode. His way of introducing new material was to add in a few new questions and try to explain them on the spot rather than introducing it first outside the game with time for guided practice.

I walked through Vince's class three times in one week: twice for under ten minutes and once for the whole period. I saw games with on-the-spot instruction all three times. Part of me wanted to tell him that I saw no teaching, no lesson steps, none of the teacher actions that lead to student learning—only fun and games. But then I thought about what he was trying to do: he was trying to make math class fun, engage more students, and build their confidence. All good ideas. He was just stuck on where to go from there: how to gamify new learning and support confidence with well-designed, collaborative practice.

To be clear: there is a place for games in mathematics. There is a place for community building and confidence building, but that place does not take up every day of the week. Still, ridiculous as some lessons may seem from the outside, nobody starts out with bad intentions; some people may just lack the tools or perspective to see how their actions need to shift to match their best intentions. Your job as a leader is to support the alignment between intention and action. Once aligned, you can support even more ambitious intentions. So, if you can't find anything nice to say about what you have observed, think again. We start with what's good so we can build on what's good.

2. *Specifying "what" and "what next."* To receive feedback and act on it, receivers need to know how you arrived at that feedback and what they are meant to do with it. That means being specific about what data was used to inform your conclusions. According to negotiation experts, Stone and Heen (2015), feedback comes from a combination of *data* (what you notice or observe) and *interpretation* (what it means to you; see Figure 6.2).

FIGURE **6.2**
Feedback: Data with Interpretation

Data	Interpretation	Data with interpretation
Everyone listened to directions.	That was a great lesson!	I thought it was great that everyone listened to directions.
Objectives weren't posted, stated, or reflected clearly by student work.	The lesson was a little unfocused.	I wasn't sure what your focus was today because objectives weren't posted, stated, or reflected clearly by student work.

Challenges arise when evaluators simply report their interpretation without explaining where it came from. Like, nice shirt.

Teachers who receive only data are also likely to be disappointed. They *want* to know your opinion, *want* to understand what you think of them, and *want* to be able to be good, great, impressive even, when you are in the room. Moreover, they *need* to know what you value and don't if they are going to practice in ways that align with those values. However, if you only share interpretation, teachers are left to guess how they earned the praise or concern you express. "Great job? What does *great job* mean?" Sharing both data *and* interpretation isn't difficult, but it is easy to forget to do so, especially when trying to balance the mountains of feelings and mountains of paperwork so often associated with observations.

3. *Being on time.* Speaking of paperwork: though many teachers report being observed more often under new-generation teacher evaluation systems, many still report that they do not regularly receive helpful feedback after being observed. Anecdotally, one common reason administrators do not follow up right away is that they are busy filling out the paperwork associated with observation, not to mention behind schedule on other things. However, we have no evidence that feedback has to come on an official form to be useful. In fact, "prompt, timely, and thorough" feedback has been associated with positive learning gains in everything from online learning to video games and professional settings (Goodwin and Miller 2012; Mory 2004; Hattie 2009). Though bombarding people with tons of immediate feedback (as in video games) may make them dependent on feedback for action, the research largely supports a sooner-and-more-specific-is-better approach (Mory 2004). This does not, however, mean that observations are no good if they aren't immediately followed by an in-person debrief session. A sticky note is enough to start.

In laboratory settings, some delay in feedback (up to three days) has been shown to support learning and memory. But, this is for tasks that participants only do every three or four days, so it means feedback was given about a task before the participant had to do the task again. After being observed, most teachers immediately teach again (sometimes the very same lesson) and continue teaching on all the days between observations and debrief conversations. So, immediate feedback respects a teacher's right to have confidence in their best work and to be thinking about their areas of improvement as soon as possible. Importantly, even in carefully controlled studies where a short delay was better than immediate feedback, both conditions were significantly better for learning and memory than no feedback (Metcalfe, Kornell, and Finn 2009).

So, it is as important to schedule time to debrief and complete paperwork for an observation as it is to schedule the observation itself. If an informal observation requires ten minutes, evaluators' calendars should block off 10–20 more minutes to write and debrief. Otherwise, we are investing all the time and energy into the part of an observation–debrief cycle that has the least to do with teacher learning. Evaluators may learn a lot by watching their teachers, but teachers gain very little from merely having a visitor in the room. Their opportunity to develop as professionals comes after—in discussions about the observation. So it makes sense to schedule and protect time and energy for feedback so that teacher–evaluator interactions can fuel improvement over time.

4. *Focusing on the future.* The easiest way to make feedback moments trust-building moments—to ensure a teacher doesn't take feedback personally or negatively—is to focus the conversation on a plan for what comes next. Observation debriefs are not opportunities for postmortem analyses of a lesson, or to show off how great you are at lesson analysis. They are a time to plan for future lessons that are more robust and powerful than the lessons that came before. Focusing on what comes next, rather than what already happened, means you have a process (and some hope!) for things to be better next time.

For example, my first semester teaching at the University of Connecticut, I got the worst course evaluations of the entire department and my entire teaching career. The open-ended comments were mostly negative, and the numeric scores, though uneven, made my average far below the mean for my department. To be fair, I teach in the department that consistently leads our campus with near-perfect evaluations every semester because we *are* the Department of Curriculum and Instruction, but it was still an unwelcomed shock.

I sat with the menacingly official manila envelope at my desk and the report spread out in front of me, unsure what to do. After a few minutes I decided to open a word document and write a note to my department chair telling her all the things I was going to do to be better next time. Panicked, I thought if I sent her a combination of apology and action plan, it would negate the judgments she was inevitably making about my potential as a professor. I was a few words in when she appeared at my door.

Casually leaning against the doorframe she said something to the effect of:

> I see you got your evaluation packet. Don't worry, the first semester is always the worst. It looks like some of the assignment guidelines were confusing and could have been clearer. Why don't you see if you can borrow syllabi from Wendy or Doug to see how they describe their assignments for next time. Let me know if you need anything else.

She smiled, and waved as she walked away.

As I look back, I realize that she:

1. Honestly sandwiched: "Don't worry, the first semester is always the worst. It looks like some of the assignment guidelines could have been clearer. Let me know if you want any other support."
2. Spoke specifically (data and interpretation): "It looks like some of the assignment guidelines were confusing and could have been clearer."
3. Came by in a timely manner: "She stopped by the day feedback was released."
4. Maintained a future orientation: "Why don't you see if you can borrow syllabi from Wendy or Doug to see how they describe their assignments for next time. Let me know if you need anything else."

I could have hugged her. What seemed like second nature to her made all the difference to me. Nothing builds trust like saying, "We're in this together." Nothing demonstrates support like already having a plan. I could trust that the advice she gave me was going to make things better, not meant to embarrass or hurt me, so I was motivated to follow it. Where I feared judgment about the past, she focused squarely on the future: I will never be new here again, my higher-scoring colleagues were there to help, and she clearly expected that I would improve.

The other feedback present in this story constitutes an example of ineffective feedback. University-level student course evaluations on their own violate all of the principles of effective feedback for learning.

~~Honestly sandwiched~~	There is no discussion (unless you have a phenomenal department chair), and there is no information about focusing on the future. Reports display feedback in the order questions appear on the student forms.
~~Specific~~	They consist of generic questions that are not specific to the course, so feedback is broad.
~~Timely~~	They come several months after the semester is over.
~~Future-oriented~~	They mainly consist of averages of several students' responses, so it is unclear what the feedback message about a given indicator should be (some people loved it, some hated it, so . . . do I do it again?).

K–12 teachers get feedback like this, too, when student scores and teacher effect scores come back from annual standardized testing midway through the summer. Printouts of teacher effect scores or overall evaluation ratings calculated by computer at some distant state office, only to be delivered months later, are often reported in isolation, without meaningful disaggregation, months after teachers can do anything with the cohort of students to which they refer. They do not come with meaningful guidance about what someone might change because they measure the outcome, not the processes, of teaching. Oddly, they may even come specified to the 100th of a point (e.g., 4.26) as if one-one-hundredth of a point means something about an individual's value. Do you know the difference between teachers with a 4.26 and a 4.27 rating? Or between a 3.9 and a 4.0? Exactly nothing.

The truth is that if these highly specified outcome scores don't mean much about the processes of teaching and learning. They may, however, have something to do with the overall success of communities of teaching and learning. They are calculated precisely so that administrators looking at teacher effects at the school and district level can see some variation in the scores and distributions of scores they use to make decisions about a building or a district, not an individual.

Knowing this, some thoughtful administrators work hard to shield teachers from the scores by keeping them, inflating them, or telling teachers to ignore them. None of these tactics meet the criteria of honesty or future orientation. Even when the data come in an unhelpful form, they can be addressed, even humanized, by a leader who provides specific, timely, sandwiched, future-orientated feedback that teachers need to use feedback as learning fuel. Or, teachers can reframe the unhelpful feedback for themselves by asking some of the questions discussed below.

Getting Feedback: Fueling Learning in the Absence of Useful Feedback

Not all feedback is good feedback. In fact, some of it is actually terrible. However, simply ignoring feedback, "even when it is off base, unfair, poorly delivered, and frankly you're not in the mood," isn't really an option for us as thinking, feeling human beings (Stone and Heen 2015, cover). Still, not all feedback is welcome, high quality, or even accurate. Some teachers have already decided that a certain evaluator or set of evaluators know nothing, have nothing to teach them, and do not have good intentions. According to Stone and Heen, it is probably more effective to teach receivers to squeeze meaning from not-so-great feedback than trying (as people in business, sports, and education have done for decades) to train people to be better at giving it. In many cases, the receiver has more control over the impact of feedback than the giver.

As a feedback receiver, you know the elements of good feedback outlined in the preceding sections are not always present. When you notice something is missing or misplaced, take action to make the feedback work for you. For example, if the feedback seems off base or unclear:

1. Ask where the feedback is coming from and where it is going: "Tell me about why you think so? What do you think is a good next step?"
2. Clarify the advice: "So does this mean I should stop doing Daily Oral Language program altogether, or just do it fewer times per week?"

You have a right to clarity, but you sometimes have to work to get it. Likewise, if you disagree with feedback, there may still be a kernel of something helpful hidden inside that you could dig for:

1. What is right about the feedback and what do you disagree with?
2. What is different about the data or interpretation you have and those of the giver?
3. Have you ever heard feedback like this before? Why has it come up again?

If the feedback might be right or wrong, but you are too upset to tell, it may be because:

1. It's too soon. That's fine. In that case, before you ask questions or beat yourself up, file the feedback so you come back to it later.

2. Notice if there is a difference between what was actually said and what you're telling yourself about what was said. This is what Stone and Heen (2015) call "separating the strands" of a feedback message.

If you're like me, you may have days where you hear a colleague joke about how you're late to a meeting and think, "I'm such a disaster, I'm always late to everything, I'm a totally irresponsible embarrassment of a person, and everyone around me knows it." Yeah. I was late once. It was funny to someone. It is not the end of the world. But, lateness is a sore spot for me and it sends me spiraling into my own stories about myself that often get reinforced. Stone and Heen hypothesize that feedback from all places is naturally woven into the stories about yourself you already carry and can set off an avalanche of thoughts and emotions that are, truly, out of proportion. I can see what they mean.

Believe it or not, it's actually a good thing that feedback can accumulate into narratives that drive us to change or help us to know ourselves better over time. But, if small pieces of feedback send you reeling, it's important to be able to take a step back and ask yourself:

1. What was actually said, and what was not said?
2. What did this make me think, and does my thinking match what was said?
3. Is this thinking a pattern for me?

Using the three questions that follow, you can reel yourself back in from hearing that the room was a little disorganized and imagining that means you're a terrible teacher. You can realize that a comment about late attendance slips is not necessarily a comment about your character, and that the fact that your department chair wants to a see a revision of your unit plan is not because they think you're bad at planning, but because they want a clean final copy. Your ability to take a step back from feedback, see it for what it is, and ask for clarification when it isn't enough may make the difference between evaluation routines that add strain and stress to an already compromised system, and those that support the learning we all need to feel good about our work.

A Measure and Sort Approach to Giving and Getting Feedback

Measure and sort approaches to feedback are focused on documenting communication to create a paper trail that can be used to build a case for promotion or dismissal. These paper trails are often online and may be guided by standard prompts, rubric language, predetermined themes/foci so that they can be viewed as objective. Such systems are useful for charting a pattern of behavior and feedback so that larger human capital decisions can be warranted. And so that those decisions stand up in court.

However, this measure and sort approach to feedback as fodder for paper trails violates three-fourths of the principles of effective feedback for learning (they may be timely, but nothing else). In addition, there is an increased likelihood of absurd errors, which threatens the trustworthiness of the system. As with canned report card comments, where some student inevitably gets a comment like "needs to work on accent" in math class rather than French class, teachers are aware that canned comments can be misfires. Moreover, though prompt, they are often not based on observed strengths (sandwiched), specific, or future-oriented.

If you work in a system where feedback has been automated in ways that do not generate learning fuel (as is so at universities), open response notes sections, actual notes, or informal conversations (like the one I had with my department chair) can engage the three missing principles while the automation ensures timeliness and keeps useful records. Keep in mind that these systems are designed to make promotion/firing decisions more straightforward and use them for this purpose, but not for generating learning fuel.

In some districts' systems, a measure and sort approach is used to track trends across classrooms within a large school or district, rather than for individual teachers. Data gathered from trend visits is usually more helpful for administrators considering a building's needs than for teachers considering their own needs. Nonetheless, trust can be lost when administrators enter classrooms to gather trend data, but say nothing to the individual teacher. So, even if you are collecting predetermined, automated data, leave a personal note or comment so that teachers know they were seen and not merely counted.

A Support and Develop Approach to Giving and Getting Feedback

A support and develop approach to feedback requires that evaluators are mindful of the human experience of feedback and the human potential for learning from feedback. Teaching is a very personal job because it is made up of a series of thousands of human interactions all day every day. Teacher evaluation really should be teach*ing* evaluation—not about the person, but about the activities and interactions that make up her classroom fabric. In my experience, even when teachers ask, "How did I do?" or "How was I?," what they really wonder is "What can I do better?" or "How can my teaching improve?"

A support and develop approach to feedback frames feedback as *joint* professional development. It starts with immediate feedback that meets the requirements above, and it continues with a discussion routine in which leaders are transparent about what they saw, what they interpret, and what they think could happen next. If, as the evaluator, you are unsure of the best next step, the teacher (and other teachers) are likely to be your best resources. If you explain the data and the interpretation (here's what I notice, here's what I wonder), colleagues, or often the teachers themselves, are likely to have a hypothesis about what to do next. Having discussions about teaching, instead of merely delivering labels of effectiveness during feedback conversations, is likely to expand your repertoire of ideas and strategies exponentially. In other words, you do not need all the answers, but you do need to be willing to ask good questions.

Key Points

- Effective feedback is honestly sandwiched, specific, timely, and future-oriented.
- Teachers can learn from ineffective feedback by taking a step back, seeing it for what it is, and ask for clarification when it isn't enough.
- Effective feedback routines constitute joint professional development: Having discussions about teaching instead expands educators' repertoires of ideas and knowledge for instruction.

Tools to Share

The following tools for Chapter 6 can be found in the appendixes:

- Structures for Framing Feedback as Learning Fuel
- Questions to Ask When You Receive Poor Feedback

7

Setting Effective Goals for Literacy Learning

> ▶ *Why is goal setting particularly difficult for literacy instruction?*
>
> ▶ *How can educators set goals that inspire, rather than restrict, ambitious teaching?*

Consider these three (paraphrased) quotes we overheard in a lunchroom conversation among teachers before we met for formal focus groups about their new teacher evaluation system:

1. Third-grade reading teacher: "I have no idea what to set for my student learning goal. Seriously. No. Idea."
2. Seventh-grade English teacher: "*You* have no idea? I don't even get to set mine! I got an email telling me what my goal is last week. It's the same for the whole grade, even the PE teacher."
3. Sixth-grade language arts teacher: "Last year I went back and forth with my supervisor six times to set a goal. Once he approved it in *December*, I'd been TWAG ("teaching without a goal") all fall. At that point, why set a goal?"

Each of these quotes demonstrates a different frustration with goal setting ranging from the difficulty of prioritizing efforts (1), to the contradictions of having a generic goal chosen for you (2), to being told your goal isn't good enough (3).

Study after study finds that having a goal (as opposed to not having one) means you will be more productive, committed, and proud of your work. So, goals, like feedback, are always assumed to be good. Yet, we know from research and experience that this simply isn't true. Goal setting is often complex, disorienting, and uncomfortable. Goals can intimidate and generate frustration just as easily as they can focus and inspire individual and collective action.

In this chapter, we describe the unique challenges of setting goals about student growth and achievement in the areas of reading and writing to highlight the specific ways literacy assessments can and cannot inform the evaluation of individual teachers. Then we discuss what goals do in any setting, serving as a form of public communication that works to focus and narrow efforts while communicating priorities.

Literacy-Specific Challenges for Setting Effective Goals

Goals based on student literacy growth or achievement have a unique set of challenges related to the way literacy is conceptualized and measured. This makes the selection of measures and interpretation of results more difficult in literacy than it is in some other areas. However, a transparent discussion of the predictable challenges of measuring growth in reading and writing can support educators in making nuanced decisions about goals that are more likely to realistically inspire, rather than restrict or frustrate teaching efforts.

Most reliable measures of reading and writing artificially constrain tasks.

If we want to know how good you are at reading and writing, we measure it in snapshots of constrained activities. To measure comprehension, we ask multiple-choice questions after students read a (short) passage and count how many times they chose the right answer. If we want to measure word recognition, we give students a leveled list of words to read and count how many times they read one incorrectly. If we want to measure fluency, we ask students to read aloud (though most reading they do in school after first grade is silent) while we time how long it takes them to finish reading a passage straight through without stopping or rereading. If we want to measure writing, we ask for a "quick write" without drafting or revising and rate it against a rubric of 5–7 indicators. Because we don't know how to objectively measure the open-ended, endlessly complex tasks we really value, we divide and constrain elements of reading and writing performance so that we can test them accurately and reliably.

Because we apply the same isolated, constrained measures to all children, the picture we create of reading and writing isn't unfair or inaccurate (quick writing is part of "real" writing; fluent reading is part of "real" reading), it is just incomplete. This effort to measure objectively and reliably also means we sometimes leave important contributors and predictors of growth out of assessment.

As researcher Peter Afflerbach (2015) notes, in addition to constraining tasks, high-stakes reading and writing tests also tend to be limited to cognitive rather than affective factors despite the outsized influence of affective factors on reading achievement. This is partially because cognitive aspects of reading (skills, strategies, and content knowledge) are easier to measure than affective aspects (self-efficacy, motivation, and engagement). But it is also because research, instruction, and assessment dollars spent since the turn of the century have been focused on the National Reading Panel's (NRP) "five pillars" of reading instruction, often to the exclusion of any other contributing factors. Affective factors did not show up in the NRP's review because it only included research published between 1976 and 2000—with all but one included study published in 1999 or earlier.

Since the turn of the twenty-first century, a critical mass of research on affective factors related to reading achievement has emerged, and in many cases eclipsed, the importance of constrained skills because of their predictive and growth-nurturing value (see Klauda and Guthrie 2015; Guthrie and Wigfield 2000). If the NRP based its findings on research from the twenty-first century (2000 and on), there is no doubt that self-efficacy, motivation, and engagement *would* be highlighted as pillars—perhaps even superpillars—next to phonics, phonemic awareness, fluency, vocabulary, and comprehension. Drawing on the surge of research on adolescent literacy published after 2000 (Carnegie Council on Advancing Adolescent Literacy 2010; Graham and Hebert 2010; Lee and Spratley 2010; Graham and Perin 2007), the NRP might have noted that phonics and phonemic awareness have less and less ability to predict overall reading, even for late-developing readers, in the middle and upper grades. A twenty-first-century reading panel might highlight the need for purposeful reading and writing activities as central to the development and coordination of individual skills, rather than identifying five distinct skill areas to develop.

As Afflerbach wrote, "Testing only skill, strategy, and content area knowledge while ignoring powerful factors such as motivation and engagement, and self-efficacy results in an incomplete portrayal of student growth . . . The incomplete account of student reading development contributes to inaccurate evaluation and misrepresentation of teachers' accomplishments" (Afflerbach 2015, 45).

Rather than assuming that assessment data "speak for themselves," or that "numbers don't lie," when it comes to assessments of reading and writing, we have to leave room for the possibility that data conceal more than they reveal about student growth, learning, and potential. For example, strategic readers might make nonsense words into real words because they are so good at drawing on multiple cueing systems to make meaning from text. Students engaged in reading a timed passage might stop to laugh, go back and reread, or comment on what they're reading, thus compromising their words-read-per-minute rate due entirely to their highly literate behavior. Strong comprehenders might have made new and interesting connections and inferences that test developers never thought to ask about and may not have noticed the details that appear in test questions.

One clear illustration of this can be found in the final reports of the Measures of Effective Teaching project (see Kane 2015). In this study, several thousand teachers were rated using different observation protocols and then their value-added scores were calculated based on two different kinds of student outcome data: state English language arts (ELA) tests, which use multiple-choice questions, and a more open-ended test of ELA, the Stanford Achievement Test, ninth edition (SAT-9). The researchers reasoned that state ELA tests were important to consider because their reliance on multiple-choice comprehension questions has a mix of higher reliability and lower validity, and that the SAT-9 offered a slight contrast because of its open-ended questions: high reliability because it is still a standardized test, and high(er) validity. Interestingly, the results of the SAT-9 were even more closely correlated with results from teacher observations no matter which observation tool was used: the Classroom Assessment Scoring System (CLASS), which measures socioemotional and academic support; the Framework for Teaching (FFT), which measures general teaching; or the Protocol for Language Arts Teaching Observation (PLATO), which measures ELA-specific practices. (See Figure 7.1.)

This finding is evidence that the more realistic open-ended assessment had even more to do with observable classroom practices than the less valid multiple-choice assessment, but both were somewhat correlated. It is also evidence that the measure itself matters—both in terms of *what* is being assessed (e.g., reading comprehension) and *how* it is being assessed. John Papay has also demonstrated this by calculating whether the reading test used and the time of year effects teacher ratings. Using existing data already collected in Massachusetts, Papay showed that many teachers who would have received bonuses based on the students' scores on a standardized

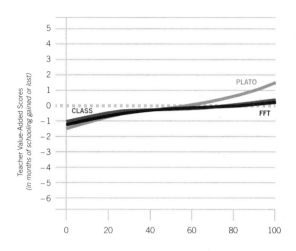

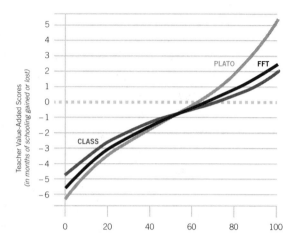

State ELA Tests   **SAT9 Open-Ended Reading Test**

FIGURE **7.1**
Correlation Between
Standardized
Assessment and Teacher
Observation Scores

test given in the fall wouldn't have received them based on their students' scores on a different assessment or even the same test given at a different time of year (Papay 2011).

All this means we use data, but do not confuse data with doctrine. We give assessments, plot the results, compare them to other sources of data, and realize that printed spreadsheets of nonsense word reading fluency, or even passage reading fluency, are partial measures of something much bigger and more important than the assessment task itself. We have the choice to prioritize construct validity (the extent to which an assessment measures what it sets out to measure) over reliability (the extent to which the test, if given again, would generate the same result). We can create complex, authentic tasks for evaluation purposes even though these are difficult to rate consistently. Or we have the ability to choose a minimally invasive assessment (like a one-minute fluency test) precisely because it is minimally invasive. In this case, we take its findings as indicators, not guarantees, of reality. There's nothing wrong with either decision, but we have to recognize the relative value of reliable, invalid data compared with valid, unreliable data: one gives a good "sense" of reading without a good measurement; the other gives good measurement without much sense.

Literacy development is unevenly distributed over time.

Patterns of growth, and even the differences in proficiency between levels, are not the same for all students or all levels. Teachers who have given the same assessment over several years will often notice that some levels seem harder to pass than others. For example, some of the passages in informal reading inventories, the Developmental Reading Assessment, second edition (DRA-2) or the Benchmark Assessment consistently stump students and others seem surprisingly easy. Likewise, students often get "stuck" in the "within-word pattern" stage of spelling development, while some might zoom (or slog) through another stage. This may not be a problem with the tests themselves; it may be an indication that it really is harder or takes longer to move between one level/stage of proficiency to the next. It may be that certain skills slowly develop while others "click" into place. Or it may be that individual students' reading habits shift because they find themselves in a series of high-engagement texts, or a rut of low-success reading experiences, and this shows in uneven patterns of growth across months and years.

So, setting a goal that all students will grow three guided reading levels, two DRA levels, or one "grade level" may mean something different for students who have different starting points. Attempting to accommodate this often looks like lowering expectations, but ignoring it might fail to honor the growth students *are* making. For example, the technical manual for the Scholastic Reading Inventory, an online assessment sometimes used as a progress-monitoring tool, reports different patterns of growth for students at different starting points. Students reading at lower levels make more growth on average than do students at upper levels.

The zillion-dollar question is "How much growth is enough?" We have several possible ways to answer this question: by comparing students to themselves, to a normed sample, or to average performance on particular tasks. None of these is perfect, but each is a perfectly plausible way to set a goal if its downsides are taken into account. The important thing is not to punish teachers for setting high expectations for themselves and their students, even if their expectations represent unprecedented growth. We know too much about the negative effect of assuming that past is prologue. A history of difficult does *not* guarantee a future with little growth. In fact, it might be exactly the opposite. Figure 7.2 provides bullet points for a discussion of the benefits and cautions for four approaches for goal setting in literacy.

Individual teachers and evaluators have the luxury of deciding how to set growth goals given these options. However, some goals are already set for us as benchmarks or cut scores that indicate proficiency. On most high-stakes assessments, the educational community assumes that

Options	Benefits	Cautions
Set goals based on expected average progress (grade levels, national norms).	Though everyone is different, individual differences will average out if you compare everyone to the mean, so you are likely to be able to claim growth overall, even if individuals do not meet the benchmark.	Students with different starting points have different distances to cover for you to meet your goal; this may mean they are not equally challenged.
Set goals based on an individual student's past performance.	Goals are differentiated so you are more likely to be able to claim growth even if it is not normative progress.	You may unnecessarily limit your expectations, and therefore inadvertently change practices.
Set goals based on trends in performance for a particular assessment.	Goals are realistic for this assessment so you are more likely to be able to claim growth if your students are similar to those with which the assessment was normed.	These are very difficult to find, even for commercially available assessments, and carry the same caution as goals based on an individual's past performance.
Set goals based on school data and priorities.	Goals are shared across teachers and may foster collective responsibility for instructional improvement.	These goals may not match the teachers' strengths and weaknesses or align to the grade level focus/content.

FIGURE **7.2**
Approaches to Setting
Growth Goals

individual differences among students balance each other and average out into a reasonable depiction of progress over time for the class as a whole. The dynamic nature of reading and writing development and the contingent nature of performance (depends on the task) also make it difficult to assign responsibility for scores to a single teacher. This tension is described in the next section.

Literacy development is distributed across in- and out-of-school experiences.

In their study of which personnel might bear the responsibility for student reading scores in a given building, Croninger and Valli (2009) found that a surprising number of adults might provide some form of reading instruction during a typical day in the life of a fourth- or fifth-grade student. Moreover, they found that this number was likely to rise just before state assessments as test preparation tasks increased. In addition, certain after-school activities, summer programs, and home or community environments might make substantial contributions to student growth over time. In fact, some researchers argue that the achievement gap among students in the middle grades can entirely be explained by summer learning loss (Alexander, Entwisle, and Olson 2007), rather than real differences in the growth students make during the school year. This does *not* mean that individual teachers don't matter, but it does mean it's illogical to award credit to one teacher when literacy may have been developed because of or despite a great many teachers (or no teacher at all) during a given period of time.

If a sibling, babysitter, or art teacher was the adult that turned a student on to the first book she loved, read under the blanket with a flashlight, and shared with a friend, isn't that person the real source of a student's scores on tests of reading achievement? If a friend who moved away, a tough decision, or the chance at a spot on a sports team was the reason a student finally connected purpose, audience, and format to write draft after draft of something meaningful, aren't the circumstances themselves responsible for the growth captured on standardized measures of writing achievement? Similarly, if a student has had access to thoughtful, individualized, high-quality instruction but has not found the right texts, resources, or reasons to engage, does that mean the teaching itself was ineffective?

Students are always learning to be literate in all different genres for all different reasons, only some of which show up on standardized tests. This is one possible explanation for the gender gap in reading achievement: the literacies girls voluntarily engage with in their leisure time may more closely mirror the literacies assessed in school settings. That doesn't mean boys have less skill, strategy, or engagement as readers and writers, it just means the kinds of reading and writing they are engaged with don't count for school. When we pin a student's reading score on a single teacher, we erase the reality that students are always developing literacies in everything they do. English, reading, or language arts teachers are conventionally assumed to be responsible for literacy development because those classes are primarily focused on text, not because they are the only place students learn to be literate.

Reading and writing aren't skills, they are coordinated accomplishments.

In a *Washington Post* op-ed, cognitive scientist Daniel Willingham wrote that "The mistaken idea that reading is a skill may be the single biggest factor holding back reading achievement in the country" (Willingham 2009). Though we can measure individual components of reading (phonics, phonemic awareness, fluency, comprehension) and writing (grammar, spelling, genre conventions, craft), holistic measures of an authentic reading or writing act are harder to come by.

Some researchers have suggested performance tasks that, like most literate tasks in the wild world outside of testing, are collaborative, goal-oriented, and complex (Hiebert, Valencia, and Afflerbach 1994). Peter Johnston described a national exam in New Zealand for which students had to work together to read, review, and evaluate titles for the school's library (Johnston 2005). They presented their choices and argued for favorites both orally and in writing by considering a set of factors related to the aspects of author's craft they had discussed in class. This task, spread out over several days, required extensive reading, writing, talking, negotiating, decision making, and persuasion. It was graded on a rubric that may not have easily separated one student's contribution from another's, but attempted to capture the coordination of reading skills and strategies (including shared reading/writing), rather than measuring them in unnatural isolation.

This is similar to the Standards-Based Change Process pioneered by Kathryn Au and Taffy Raphael, in which teachers spend significant amounts of time articulating what it would look like for students to be engaging in literacy at each grade level and what it would take to get there (see Raphael, Au, and Goldman 2009). Goal setting then revolves around creating the conditions and contexts for students to enact literate practices, not on the scores students earn. Their focus is on the *"process of becoming"* (Raphael, Au, and Goldman 2009, 205) great readers and writers, not on interim outcome measures.

Also in the United States, the portfolio movement (see Valencia, Hiebert, and Afflerbach 2004) is the closest example of an effort to keep students engaged in the kinds of reading and writing processes we want them to acquire for college and career while gathering evidence of their growth. Instead of stopping instruction to assess using piecemeal snapshots of individual components of reading, students read, write, and talk for different reasons while teachers work to observe changes and opportunities for instruction. Artifacts of students' engagement with literate practices are collected and analyzed over time to add dimension to the "snapshots" assessments provide. The difficulty then, is not in deciding whether growth occurred, but whether the growth was normative: Is it the same as the average expected growth of all peers? Is it the same as expected benchmarks for a given grade? Is this child's change good enough?

The push for more data in schools seems mostly to have led to elaborate systems that collect impoverished sources of information about students as readers and writers. For reading alone, schools may have universal screens, progress-monitoring tools, formative assessments, state tests, and the occasional teacher-created quiz even before a teacher sits down to set a "SMART" goal (specific, measurable, alignable, realistic, time-related) that may require they create yet another data stream.

In an ironic twist, in 2014, the federal government began offering grants for "assessment reduction" so that students spend more time learning and less time testing. Ironically, the evaluation of teachers (another policy signature of 2014 in some states) has often generated the need for more, rather than fewer, assessments so that teachers have data to demonstrate their effects on student achievement. The goal of assessment in the era of accountability is to maximize value while minimizing time spent on assessments. That means: pick your battles.

How to Set and Evaluate Effective Goals for Literacy Learning

When educators set goals, they should inspire, not restrict, ambitious teaching. Because goal setting is always a delicate balancing act for competing forces, and is *never* as simple as it seems, we suggest a small set of paired questions to guard against goals with unintended negative consequences:

Paired Questions for Effective Goal Setting in Literacy

1. Is this goal based on a measure that matters? If not, is it manageable enough to stay out of the way of meaningful work?
2. Does this goal inspire high expectations? If not, are there other indications that expectations are high?
3. Does this investment in data production, collection, and analysis benefit students in any way? If not, can other measures be used instead?

Goals focus and narrow efforts.

Goals can function as tools that indicate importance, magnetize resources to a particular area, and focus attention. For example, if you set a goal to make it home by 6 PM every day, you prioritize your resources (time, money, attention) to make sure that you do, even if that means deprioritizing other things. Having this goal indicates to other people that arriving home by 6 PM is important to you, and they may want or need to change their behavior or priorities to accommodate it.

In a classroom, I might set a goal to ask students to provide evidence with their answers instead of accepting the first thing they say. This means I will be spending time and attention on this practice while probably letting go of another (like calling on as many students as possible). This goal indicates to others that I am investing in higher-order thinking and discussion, so they are likely to think of me when topics or resources related to this arise. This might mean I hear about articles, resources, or questions other teachers have about higher-order discussion strategies, but I might not hear about other things.

I might also, like many educators across America, set a goal that my students' fluency will increase by a certain number of words per minute this year. The words per minute may be based on nationally normed grade-level expectations, but it's no guarantee that students will understand, use, share, learn, or like what they read so quickly and smoothly. It may mean that I spend time and attention on reading quickly and smoothly, that I attend a fluency workshop on a professional development day, and that my school invests in an online fluency program for me and my grade-level team. None of these things is likely to directly lead to meaningful literacy growth, so I could decide to choose differently.

Instead of focusing on reading quickly and smoothly, I could use my knowledge of literacy to infer that investments in wide reading, opportunities to perform texts (rehearse, recite, even memorize), and high-success, engaged reading experiences support fluency (among other things). I might invest time and attention ensuring students spend a large amount of the period reading a variety of text types on an optimal level for growth. I might attend workshops for events like Poetry Out Loud, or I might dramatize some content and allow students to read/write and perform skits about it. Colleagues would be likely to share texts that can be read in pairs, out loud and/or over the loudspeaker, and my administration might invest in an app that lets students record their rehearsed readings of children's books and poetry for students in the younger grades. All these efforts are likely to lead to meaningful literacy growth—as measured by fluency tests—but they require much more than reading quickly and smoothly.

Goals communicate priorities.

Far from being obviously helpful or positive, goal setting is inherently dilemmatic in nature: competing interests push/pull the scope and focus of an individual's goals in ways that can create tension and confusion. Do you set a goal you *wish* you could achieve, or one you *know* you could achieve?

Do you focus on students you're confident will grow, or on those with a history of difficulty demonstrating growth? Do you believe you can be the teacher who makes significant gains with this particular set of students, whether or not anyone has done it before? Or do you stay safe and set a goal you know you can achieve because you have other things to worry about?

Educators are often not encouraged to set goals individually or in private the way we might with a New Year's resolution, or a personal commitment to eating fewer jelly beans. So, we also have to manage perceptions about our ambition even as we manage the focus and measurement of our goals. Ambition, like pride, is one of those things of which it's good to have some, but not too much. People judge you for not being ambitious enough ("Don't you believe all children can learn?") and for being too ambitious ("Who do you think you are, a miracle worker?").

Before we even think about the content of a teacher's goal, the structure of the goal already contains dilemmas. Should they be set by individuals or groups? Should they be selected by teachers or administrators or both? Should there be strict guidelines or should they be organic? The answer to most of these questions is: yes, a little bit of both. Too far in one direction (e.g., always individual or always group goal setting) restricts progress by limiting what goals can be used to do. Group goals allow for collaboration but individual goals may be more personally inspiring. Individual goals differentiate to optimize buy-in and personal growth. There is always a need to balance the potential of different goal structures and/or to leave room for more than one if goals are going to inspire, rather than restrict, ambitious teaching.

There isn't a wrong answer, but choices can feel wrong when they are made without considering what each one offers as a tool for focusing efforts and communicating priorities.

Varying Goals Over Time to Maximize Effectiveness

So far, this chapter has focused on the realities that make goal setting complicated and imperfect no matter what you do. You cannot generate an authentic assessment for every aspect of literacy you care about for every student every year. But you can prioritize one holistic measure, one area to pursue self-study, at some point in a year or set of years. Because no way is the perfect way, and setting multiple goals at once often limits their potential to focus efforts, the best solution is to vary the goals you set *over time* so that you can have the benefit of varied approaches over time.

To leave room for different kinds of goals and different mechanisms of support, one district in Connecticut created a three-year cycle for teacher evaluation in which teachers rotate between three phases of evaluation activities. In the first year (and for all new teachers on provisional licenses), teachers set goals based on school goals and initiatives and go through the typical observation cycle. If they earn proficient scores, they may be released to do self-study or independent inquiry for a year. During a release year, their goals match their own area of inquiry, and they have time and resources dedicated to pursuing an independently selected area for improvement. They are evaluated based on the progress they make in this, instead of every, area. The third year is an opportunity for focused collaboration in the form of lesson study, peer review, or small-group instructional rounds. For this year only, evaluation activities are bound in focused collaboration activities. Then, the cycle repeats.

Though this best-of-all-worlds three-year cycle is not a fit for every setting, several other districts in the state have or will attempt variations on the theme. Some keep evaluation activities the same year to year, but change the focus and type of goals within their static system. Still, the three-year cycle stands as an example of the possibility of maximizing different approaches to goal setting (idealistic vs. realistic; individual vs. group) by using each for its intended purpose at some point in the cycle. This may be something individual teacher–evaluator dyads decide among themselves each year, or something a bit more formalized, like the expectation that goals will vary every few years to ensure teachers are focusing on different aspects of instruction, different avenues for growth, over time.

A Measure and Sort Approach to Setting Effective Goals

A measure and sort approach to addressing the inherent dilemmas in goal setting would minimize difficulty setting goals by making goal setting a simple, straightforward task that doesn't take up time or resources. This means setting them at a building, grade, or team level without much discussion or many changes over time. Goals would be measured using existing measures whenever possible, even if the measures are not particularly aligned with the goal. For example, if the goal is to "make 1.5 years' worth of growth in reading" the school might use state test scores (multiple choice) or universal screens (fill in the missing word on leveled passages) even though these are limited snapshots of what students can do on a given day. Still, because these are already in use in many schools, they add no time and take no attention away from other instructional tasks, and they leave a lot of room for teachers to choose areas to focus their time and attention while still meeting the goal.

In these settings, teachers may not think about their goals throughout the year and may not use these goals to focus their efforts and resources. By the end of the year, they are likely to be able to reach these goals without difficulty so that the goal-setting process and end-of-year rating do not take any energy away from their teaching.

After goals are monitored, teachers can be sorted based on whether or not they reach particular goals. However, because the measure of a big goal like overall reading achievement is likely to feel disconnected from the everyday routines, tools, and strategies teachers employ, such measures can't provide key insights for improving instruction, but they also won't get in the way of instruction. The measure and sort approach prioritizes clean, easily collectable data and interprets the data in measured ways so that inferences are limited and time is preserved for other instructional and professional endeavors. In other words, if we divest energy in goal setting, we can't give data gathered for goal monitoring the same weight when making decisions about teacher effectiveness or professional development.

A Support and Develop Approach to Setting Effective Goals

A support and develop approach to goal setting would invest in the opportunity for individual teachers to reflect, refine a focus for their own development, and invest resources in developing that area. This might look like an independent inquiry project or a collaborative project aimed at improving a certain unit, practice, or approach. It invests in the process of teaching, rather than the outcome. This releases educators from comparing students to their pasts or others' performance and uses assessment as a tool for learning, rather than measurement. Where the goal is measurement, this choice is inappropriate. However, where the goal is development, this choice allows teachers to concentrate on extending students' competence as far as they can without being limited by assumptions about potential.

- Goals focus and narrow effort, attention, importance, and the distribution of resources.
- Most measures of reading and writing artificially constrain tasks or criteria to increase reliability. This fact of reading/writing assessment requires intentional framing and balancing when scores are used as a measure of teacher effectiveness.
- Literacy development is widely distributed over time and across settings. This fact of literacy development requires specific measures with meaningful benchmarks when student growth is used as a measure of teacher effectiveness.

Tools to Share

The following tool for Chapter 7 can be found in the appendixes:

- Goal Envisioning Worksheet

Evolving Policies to Improve Teaching

> ▶ *How can the teaching profession strengthen itself within and outside of accountability policies?*

Kudzu is an invasive weed that annually winds its vines around the trees and telephone poles that line most roads and highways in Knoxville, Tennessee, where we both went to school. Kudzu offers a lot of environmental benefits like protecting soil from erosion and infusing it with nitrogen, but is also associated with significant environmental and ecological damage because of what scientists call "interference competition"—it outcompetes other species for resources, killing most other plants in its path.

Kudzu was originally brought into the United States as an ornamental vine, but during the Great Depression, the federal government paid farmers in southeastern states to plant as much of the soil-enriching groundcover as they could. Back then, they called it "the miracle vine" and thought it would aid conservation and crop production. That is, until it spread. Now, the *New York Times* and others call it "the vine that ate the south," because endless sheets of its green leaves can be found literally everywhere, squeezing out whatever lived there before.

Creative efforts to curb the continuous growth of the now ubiquitous weed have included everything from experimental chemical compounds to flocks of civic-minded goats freely grazing along the highways. As residents of affected areas know, the challenge of living with kudzu is finding a way to embrace what it offers while guarding against its invasive patterns of growth.

And so it is with accountability policies. They come with good intentions, offer some benefits, but also crowd out other things and can stifle that which they are designed to support.

As stewards of the profession of education, teachers and leaders must aim to squeeze the benefits out of evaluation policies, while creatively restricting their hold on other kinds of growth. As we have described across chapters in this book, there are ways to benefit from potentially invasive policies that threaten to stifle as much as they support.

First, we must make use of the structure evaluation policies offer. Teacher evaluation policies parallel other school and district accountability policies by requiring individual and collective goals, data collection, analysis, and data-driven decision making. They create a need for collegial collaboration and communication between teachers and leaders. This can create "interference competition" in places where such things were already underway in different forms, or it can provide cover for those budding ideals and initiatives that need a structure in which to thrive. In other words, evaluation processes like goal setting can focus attention on the plans, hopes, and ideals that teachers and leaders bring to their work. Or, they can distract from efforts already underway to realize those hopes and ideals. So, instead of viewing evaluation efforts as a competitive force, ruthlessly consuming resources meant for other things, the routines associated with evaluation can be borrowed and put to use for the goals of the individual and the school.

Second, we must work for coherence and clarity by (re)framing the purpose of policies in each local context. Teacher evaluation systems stifle growth and development when messages about the purposes of each activity are mixed. If the goals of evaluation activities are not transparent—if teachers approach goal setting from a support and develop orientation only to be met with a measure and sort response—there is interference competition for trust, growth, and development. If teachers and leaders agree on their approach for each activity, their efforts are more likely to converge and contribute to trust, growth, and professional learning.

Assumptions and Realities of Teacher Evaluation Policies

As laid out in Chapter 1, the purpose of evaluation policy is to hold teachers accountable for demonstrating particular practices and making a certain level of progress with the underlying assumption that this will boost achievement and improve educational outcomes, particularly for underserved students.

Even though improved teaching and learning are the explicit goals of teacher evaluation policies, less than one-third of the indicators included on most available rubrics for evaluation are actually focused on instruction. Similarly, within evaluation legislation, almost no legislative language and literally no funding are focused on the development of teaching practice. Instead, policies are aimed at creating the infrastructure for evaluation activities: protocols, procedures, and data systems that identify who knows/ needs to know more. In most cases, states assume that generating more data about teachers will "inform" better professional development (PD). Some even go as far as mandating that PD be explicitly linked to evaluation data. This is both good news and bad news.

It is good news that teachers may be subjected to less whole-school, undifferentiated "PD" opportunities if the expectation is that PD activities match individual needs. It is bad news because it is unclear what (if anything) has emerged to fill this new expectation of individualized PD. In some cases, a vending machine model of PD has emerged in which districts buy into an online evaluation management system that has videos and online modules attached to each rubric indicator. In these settings, low scores on one row of the rubric trigger an automatic invitation to watch videos and complete an online module on the topic. The assumption is that doing so will improve a teacher's rating. "Plug and chug" your professional growth.

Beyond these vending machine models, schools and districts have moved slowly to match PD to evaluation ratings. This is mostly due to the intensity of establishing new evaluation systems causing "interference competition" with other PD efforts. Such interference is compounded by the catch-22 of needing to plan PD a year or more in advance, leaving little room for flexible responses to emerging needs.

Finally, it is unclear whether the focus of evaluation instruments is sufficient for identifying PD needs. That is, whether or not rubrics focus on the aspects of practice that are the right grain size, or the most powerful, most important, or most realistic for teachers and leaders to address within PD structures. As we discussed in Chapter 5, there is no empirical evidence that teacher evaluation systems have improved the equity or quality of instruction, though there is some evidence that they support more conversations about teaching than would otherwise occur and that this leads to temporary, modest gains in high-performing schools (Steinberg and Sartain 2015).

There is also solid evidence that new-generation teacher evaluation systems fail to differentiate teacher quality, partly because of human error and partly because of how they are organized to average, round up, or matrix out scores in different domains. It becomes statistically difficult to earn a score that is far from the mean (either very high or very low) when observation scores are only one of many measures averaged or added together to create an overall rating (Amrein-Beardsley et al. 2015). And, though there is some variation in teacher performance, the idea that there were throngs of "ineffectives" lurking around every neighborhood school, quietly teaching badly, has been debunked (Gabriel 2015). Very few teachers ever actually earn the lowest available ratings under new-generation policies even after evaluators have been trained and retrained to rate objectively. So, if teacher evaluation is going to be used to increase overall teacher effectiveness, it has to do more than identify teachers for elimination; it has to be part of an ecology in which teachers might thrive.

Making Teacher Evaluation Work for You

Given the imbalance in resources aimed at accountability vs. support, new policies could invest in development efforts, while potentially divesting the aspects of accountability that constrain collaboration and compete for educators' attention. For example, rather than buying subscriptions to PD management systems online, schools might allocate funds for (some) teachers to select a learning experience aimed at an individual area for growth. Teachers might all choose different formats and topics for PD, but this might be the most appropriate (and least restrictive) approach to differentiation.

Instead of investing in training and retraining evaluators to generate more "objective and reliable" ratings, new policies might invest in trainings aimed at increasing the instructional knowledge base of evaluators so that they see more (not less) in classroom observations and have a wider range of resources from which to draw suggestions for teachers. Likewise, instead of evaluating a teacher annually despite a history of consistently high ratings, new policies might release a teacher from evaluation activities to either engage in their own PD activity or support new teachers using the hours and funding that would have been spent confirming known effectiveness.

New policies could also decouple domains of teaching so that they are not averaged together as equals in an overall rating. For example, instead of averaging teacher ratings in the domains of instruction, planning, professionalism, and assessment or instruction, student achievement, parent surveys, and so on, new policies could report scores in each area so that relative needs could be prioritized. That way being a good citizen and a friendly colleague cannot cover up the need for growth in the area of instruction. Similarly, strong student achievement scores would no longer mask the need to continuously improve instruction if the domains of instruction and achievement were reported individually.

In other words, rather than addressing accountability and support in a single policy, where most funding is shunted toward accountability with the assumption that support will somehow follow, new policies could flip this coin. New policies could invest in infrastructure for high-quality professional learning opportunities and divest in the many ornate measurement tools that frustrate and duplicate each other's efforts (see Appendix 8A).

Additionally, new or revised policies could include an extended timeline for rollout (e.g., two or three years, rather than one). This would give teachers and leaders time to learn about new systems, procedures, and routines and to shift organizational culture and individual mind-set over time, rather than jarring a faculty into a new system in the space of a single staff meeting. Finding ways to embrace and curb the kudzu of new policies takes time, knowledge, and some trial and error. So, incremental shifts may do more to support teacher learning and student achievement than giant earthquakes will.

Shifting the Focus of Evaluation

We've all heard talk about needing more professional development, more professional texts and resources, and more time for professional learning communities, yet these structures seem "necessary, but not sufficient" for improvement efforts. We also know more isn't always better and that too many PD efforts fall short of best practices for adult learning *and* organizational change. Large-scale studies of change in school settings have demonstrated that there are predictable "levels of use" for a new innovation and predictable "stages of concern" for those adjusting to something new (Southwest Educational Development Lab 2016). To address concerns and progress toward learning and development, both teachers and schools as organizations may need to reorient to change. First, teachers could demonstrate openness to change by asking questions, building context from multiple sources, and taking risks (large or small) to show that they are critically engaged, not recalcitrant. Second, schools, as organizations, could "open up" so that they can learn about what's working—and not working—and move rapidly to improve. That means seeking feedback from teachers early and often, considering the sources of perceived roadblocks and concerns, and visibly supporting the risks (large or small) teachers take in their lessons and collaboration together. When teachers and schools are open to learning and change, they are reflective and adaptable, and they take risks individually and collectively.

By focusing on content-specific, high-quality instruction and teacher development, evaluation systems and practices can play a role in creating this mind-set. High-quality PD attends to context, provides space for questioning and testing, and leaves room for feedback. This could catapult teaching from the category of service to that of a profession with collective expertise, with implications for teacher recruitment, education, and retention. Additionally, this could reduce the simultaneous "too-muchness" and "more is better" attitude toward professional development and raise the bar on the quality of professional learning opportunities. These learning opportunities would be contextualized, engaging, and even challenging. They would match particular teachers' needs and focus on the core work of schools: teaching and learning.

Looking Ahead to the Future

The wave of new-generation teacher evaluation policies began building significant strength in 2009, peaked over the next five years, and has already begun to settle into its permanent position. Since 2013, high-profile reports, lawsuits, and grassroots advocacy efforts have destabilized the authority of statistical measures of teacher effectiveness like value-added measurement. Special interest stories in the news and testimonials before legislatures have highlighted the folly of certain aspects of initial policies (like applying the same rubric to first-grade teachers and high school counselors), and almost all of the forty-six states with new-generation policies have considered and/or passed revisions to their policies that roll back the threat of removing tenure (e.g., New York), revise the importance of value-added data in calculating an overall rating (e.g., Tennessee), and leave room for more than one observation rubric to be used across grades, schools, and staff positions (e.g., Connecticut).

Though the edges may have softened, the basic structure of new-generation teacher evaluation systems have survived their first round of revision and are likely to remain in place for a long time. The argument of this book has been that teachers and leaders *can* make evaluation systems work for them, but that these systems are not always designed or implemented with support and development in mind. As observations and measures of student growth become taken-for-granted features of teaching and learning in U.S. public schools, we have a responsibility to use them well, not only as tools for accountability, but as tools for growth. In addition, we have a responsibility to build on the possibilities of open classroom doors, frequent conversations about teaching, and a common language for what counts as effectiveness in all of our efforts to recruit, prepare, and mentor new teachers in the profession.

The accountability movement has already reached into teacher preparation programs, where accrediting bodies require all the same things of preservice teachers that school leaders require of inservice teachers: observations, goals, measures of student growth, and so on. Though several years behind the timeline of such efforts in K–12 schools, teacher recruitment, preparation, and mentoring programs can learn from the lessons of K–12 schools. They must tend their own kudzu to ensure teachers thrive as a result of their engagement with evaluation activities, rather than despite it.

As Pat Summitt (and Abraham Lincoln) said: "It is what it is, but it will be what you make it." We hope you make evaluation work for you.

Tools to Share

The following tool for Chapter 8 can be found in the appendixes:

- Rubric for Identifying High-Quality Professional Development

Resources to Support Policy Knowledge

Use this chart to fill in national, regional, and local sources of information about education issues, trends, and policies. Start with those listed below and chat with colleagues to find a mix of media and perspectives for your area so you can see all sides of an issue.

National	↔	Regional	↔	Local
Listservs and Digests	**Podcasts**	**Blogs**	**Twitter**	**Newsletters**
EdWeek Updates	NPR Ed	Vamboozled.com	U.S. Department of Education	*Reading Today*
ASCD Smartbriefs	Educate (American Public Media)	Dianeravitch.net	Diane Ravitch	Local union mailings
The Marshall Memo	Education gadfly show	This Week in Education	Heinemann	
National Education Policy Center	Edchat radio	Schools Matter	Your state representative(s)	
		The Quick and the Ed	#Edchat	
			#schoolreform	
			#occupyeducation	
			#usedgov	
			#policy4results	
			#edpresssec	

Process for Becoming Informed About Policy

We propose a multistep process for becoming informed about education policy:

1. Find *original* policy documents (often linked on state Department of Education or district websites). Hint: use the bill name/number (e.g., HB270) as a search term.

    a. Use, but do not rely on, summaries of legislation provided by state or third-party sources—these are often summarized in ways that promote an agenda and limit your view of the full policy (see Garan 2002, 2004 for examples of this).

    b. Full policy documents may seem intimidating because they are long, formal, and often include multiple items of legislation in one package. The formal language becomes predictable/repetitive (and therefore skimmable!). Try searching a keyword you care about to see where it's mentioned, or using the table of contents to isolate the sections you are most interested in.

2. Read, listen, watch media coverage on education policy.

    a. Sign up for automatic updates (ASCD SmartBrief, EdWeek Update, Marshall Memo, National Education Policy Center updates, and others).

    b. Subscribe to alerts from blogs that focus on issues in your state/grade/content area.

3. Cut through the rhetorical fireworks so that you can access the arguments without being attacked by the writer's emotions.

    a. Skim adjectives and question inflammatory word choices so that you can see the storyline behind all the political spectacle.

    b. Ask yourself: Why was this writer motivated to write about this topic in this way? What does he have to gain/lose?

    c. What about this information and argument have I heard before? What is new to me?

4. Reflect on the overlap and divergence of policy documents with media representations.

    a. Who is on what side?

    b. What other issues or debates does this remind you of?

    c. How does a new policy connect to existing policies and programs?

5. Connect what you know about your setting, your leaders, and your practice with the policy documents and media coverage.

    a. What resonates? What doesn't?

    b. Why might the media representation and your experience differ?

6. Talk with your colleagues.

    a. Ask questions to see what colleagues have heard and read within their own personal and professional networks.

    b. Respond to rumors using what you've learned by comparing sources with those who have heard something else.

7. Share what you find.

    a. Consider emailing, listing, or posting the information you found most relevant so that others can start there with their own research.

    b. Pinterest boards and Thinglink.com boards are easy ways to compile and share online resources.

Influences on Classroom Practice Discussion Starter

The chart below shows some potential influences on classroom practice. Discuss with colleagues:

- What else would you add?
- Which are the three most influential at the moment?
- Which are currently in conflict/alignment?

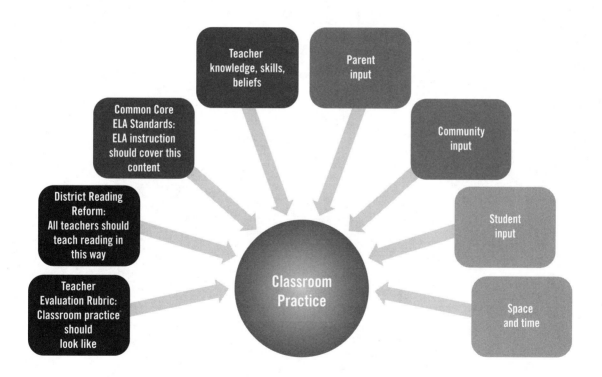

© 2017 by Rachael Gabriel and Sarah Woulfin, from *Making Teaching Evaluation Work*. Portsmouth, NH: Heinemann.

APPENDIX 2A

Initiative Alignment Tool

Most school reforms, programs, and initiatives are loosely aimed at increasing student achievement or school climate. Use this chart (row one is an example) to identify areas of overlap between concurrent initiatives.

Initiative	Short-Term Goal	Long-Term Goal	Tools	Processes
Summer Reading	Make sure more kids read over the summer	Increase reading levels/stem summer reading loss	Summer reading guidebook Online reading logs Prizes and awards assembly	Students set goals for summer reading in June Students use online reading logs June–Aug. Teachers track volume of reading in Sept.

Evaluation Tool Cost and Benefit Discussion Starter

Use the table below, reproduced from Chapter 2, to begin a discussion of the particular costs and benefits of the tools used in your school.

- Do some costs/benefits depend on the grade, subject, or other job assignment?
- Do some educators have differing opinions about the relative value of each component?
- Which benefits could be highlighted or maximized?
- Which costs could be addressed or minimized?

Component	Costs	Benefits
Rubrics	• Are one size fits all, so they are not differentiated to account for subject area or grade level? • Provide time to learn the language/principles of the rubric	• Provide a consistent framework for observing instruction
Observation Debriefs	• Require coordination of time between administrator and teacher	• Enable administrators and teachers to discuss and reflect upon classroom practice
Goals and Student Learning Objectives	• Emphasize particular forms of assessment • Narrow the focus of efforts in particular areas	• Permit teachers to set focal areas for improvement
Surveys and Whole-School Metrics	• Provide general, undifferentiated feedback	• Provide information on the school as a whole

Things to Look For/Questions for Discussion About Environments and Resources for Literacy in Your School

The following tools are designed to be used by teachers, coaches, or other instructional leaders to take stock of existing resources, materials, and conditions supportive of high-quality, engaging literacy instruction. We encourage individuals and groups to respond to these questions, seek out additional information to answer these questions, and consider the presence and absence of other materials, as well as the reasons how or why those materials are in the school/classroom.

Things to look for/questions to ask about environments for literacy instruction:

In Classrooms

- How do students access texts?

- How is reading tracked or measured?

- What types of texts are visible in the classroom?

- In what ways do the books match students' backgrounds and interests?

- How are textbooks/core reading programs used?

In Grade-Level Teams

- Where are books stored?

- Who has access to the book room?

- Who manages/organizes the book room?

- What is the process for requesting new books?

- What outside partners (libraries, district offices, unions, nonprofit organizations) offer sources of texts we can use?

- What are the expectations for procuring books, organizing classroom libraries, and sending books home with students?

- What online resources are available?

- What is the process for requesting other online resources?

Questions for Discussion About Classroom and School Libraries

- How many texts are available for students?
- How many students are enrolled in the class/school?
- How many students are currently using these books?
- Is there an adequate number of texts available for students, teachers, the school? How do you know?
- What are the most represented formats? Genre? Level? Least represented?
- Do texts represent a variety of genres, levels, and formats?
- What percent of books reflect students' backgrounds and interests? How do you know?
- What types of texts would students read more of if they were available? How do you know?
- What barriers to access currently exist (e.g., library hours, book storage, book display, online barriers, student awareness)?

Cycles of Reading Success/Failure

Cycles of Reading *Growth*

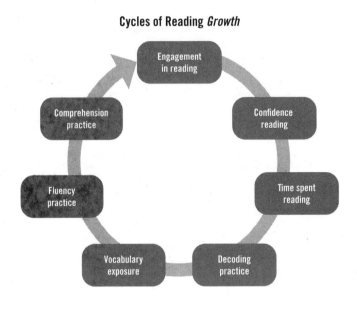

Cycles of Reading Failure

Allocated Versus Actual Timekeeper

Administrators, coaches, teachers, students, and even student teachers, interns, or volunteers can help keep track of allocated versus actual time for literacy, or for each active ingredient of literacy (see Chapter 4). Though you may not need to see literate activity 100 percent of the time, conversations about how time is spent, and whether it is being spent as intended, can be valuable for planning and understanding the rhythm of instruction across grades and classrooms.

Mins.	Allocated Describe how this time will be used	Actual Describe how this time was used
0–10		
10–20		
20–30		
30–40		
40–50		
50–60		
60–70		
70–80		
80–90		

Questions for Discussion

- How closely do allocated and actual times match?
- How often do you think this match occurs? (Is today usual, unusual, a periodic occurrence?)
- What factors most often interrupt time allocated for literacy?
- What factors support the use of time allocated for literacy?

Criteria for Quality Sources of Online Texts

Sources need not meet all criteria listed below, but the more the better!

- Are the texts interesting (e.g., up to date, on relevant topics, related to current culture)?
- Is there a range of levels available?
- Are the texts leveled and searchable by level?
- Can students choose the text (or is it selected for them)?
- Can students read texts in any order?
- Can students read texts without interruption?
- Are there questions/quizzes?
- Can students read without answering the questions/quizzes?
- Are there built-in supports for understanding (e.g., definitions, voice-overs, images, links to outside sources)?
- Is there a social component (e.g., interaction with other readers, score comparisons with other readers)?
- Are texts presented with few distracting ads, animated features, and additions?

Sources of Leveled Texts Online

New York Times Kids blog
http://www.nytimes.com/section/learning

Tween Tribune
http://tweentribune.com/

Epic Books
https://www.getepic.com/

Kids Discover
http://www.kidsdiscover.com/quick-reads/
(nonfiction focus)

Common Lit
http://www.commonlit.org/
(comes with discussion questions but unleveled)

ReadWorks
http://www.readworks.org/

Starfall
http://www.starfall.com/n/level-c/index/play.htm?f

Breaking News English
http://www.breakingnewsenglish.com/

For the teachers
http://www.fortheteachers.org/reading_skills/

ThinkCERCA
http://www.thinkcerca.com/

NewsELA
https://newsela.com/

News in Levels
http://www.newsinlevels.com/

Unite for Literacy
http://www.uniteforliteracy.com/

Bookbox
https://www.youtube.com/user/bookboxinc

Center for the Study of Adult Literacy
http://csal.gsu.edu/content/are-you-learner

Coaches as Partners in Evaluation

Below you will find an overview of the potential role of literacy coaches and other specialized literacy professionals in teacher evaluation processes with embedded questions for discussion.

Coaches are leaders who can help align the puzzle pieces of evaluation policies and English language arts (ELA) instruction for teachers, as well as school and district leaders. We note that it is beneficial for coaches to hold a deep understanding of the structure and focus of ELA policies and programs, including teacher evaluation policies, of their district and state. As such, coaches should study state instructional frameworks and district reading plans to identify key branches. Then coaches can share these understandings and connections in clear and engaging ways with teachers to support coherence and common ways of understanding not only what policies require, but why. This could be embedded in professional learning community sessions or even one-on-one conversations with teachers. Coaches can also broach conversations with district and school administrators about how to prioritize certain pieces of the reading program given particular policies and initiatives. These discussions can contribute to a shared vision for literacy.

- How do you learn about evaluation policy?
- How do you learn about district and state frameworks/approaches for ELA?

Additionally, although coaches are not involved in evaluating teachers, we still urge coaches to dig into the details of evaluation systems so that they can serve as a resource for teachers as they navigate evaluation systems. With the proper information, coaches can answer teachers' questions and support teachers in linking effective literacy instruction with the demands of evaluation. If coaches have a clear idea of the demands of teacher evaluation rubrics and standards, they can coach teachers toward practices that evaluators will recognize. This will ensure teachers do not get mixed messages from coaches and evaluators because the goals of coaching and evaluation will be in alignment.

- What types of questions do teacher raise to you about evaluation?
- How do you support teacher learning about ELA? About the evaluation system and process?

We also encourage coaches and evaluators to meet to reflect upon the match between their messaging on evaluation and literacy instruction. This collaboration can raise administrators' awareness of the ways that literacy and evaluation efforts fit together.

© 2017 by Rachael Gabriel and Sarah Woulfin, from *Making Teaching Evaluation Work*. Portsmouth, NH: Heinemann.

- What is the nature of your collaboration with school and district administrators?

- To what degree do your administrator and you share a common vision for literacy instruction and outcomes?

Ways to Learn About Evaluation in Your Context

Sit in on a meeting where teachers are setting goals and see what approaches seem to work, what questions come up, and how school assessment practices help or hinder this work.

Shadow an evaluator or sit in on a rubric training or norming session so that you can see what evaluators are looking for during classroom observations.

Create a crosswalk document that illustrates how your school's literacy practices or initiatives connect to specific schoolwide goals or rubric rows.

Ultimately, the best way to be positioned as a resource for teachers and administrators working within a teacher evaluation system is for coaches to use each of the tools of the system for themselves. For this reason, we present the crosswalk of coaching and the stages of evaluation.

In many schools, coaches carry out some form of observations inside teachers' classrooms. Yet coaches' observations may be quite different than the observations carried out by administrators. At the same time, we share that there are ways for coaches to model focusing on principles of instruction. In particular, coaches can observe and provide feedback in ways that attend to the key components of literacy instruction. Coaches who conduct observations should be mindful of the central principles of effective feedback, as discussed in Chapter 6. They should strive to give teachers clear, actionable, and prompt feedback. We acknowledge that, because the coach juggles numerous responsibilities, it may prove challenging to find the one-on-one time to give feedback to teachers. However, this prompt feedback is crucial so the coach maintains the teacher's trust and develops teacher capacity. Coaches, too, should listen and learn while providing feedback to teachers. During this stage, coaches should be clear about norms of confidentiality regarding feedback to teachers.

- Reflect upon the strengths and limitations of your recent observation and feedback cycles:
  » What are some strategies that you use so that teachers receive clear, actionable, and prompt feedback?

  » What are some challenges for you to provide this type of feedback? What could support you in overcoming those challenges?

  » How do you communicate with teachers about your stance toward confidentiality?

By bringing teachers together to study and discuss their district's formal rubric, coaches can work with teachers on developing a common vocabulary around high-quality instruction. In this manner, coaches can raise teachers' understanding of the bands of the observation rubric, which, in turn, could yield more productive feedback conversations for teachers and leaders. As a result, there can be greater coherence among teachers, coaches, and other leaders.

- How do you develop teachers' knowledge related to the evaluation rubric?

Coaches can also collaborate with teachers on setting and reaching goals. Specifically, after developing teachers' understanding of the goal-setting process, coaches and teachers can draft goals and brainstorm activities to attain those goals.

- How do you develop teachers' knowledge and skills related to goal setting?

Because coaches are *not* administrators, they can play an important role in teaching teachers about evaluation. Coaches are well positioned to talk through the steps, benefits, and concerns of a district's evaluation system with teachers in a way that those formally observing may not be able to. The coach–teacher dialogue on the observation process can be positive for teachers, as well as the school system. By opening lines of communication about observations, coaches can raise the curtain, demystifying the realm of evaluation and tying it to crucial pillars of literacy instruction.

- Reflect upon the strengths and limitations of your communication around evaluation policy and literacy instruction:
  » What areas of literacy instruction have your recent professional development sessions for teachers addressed?
  » How could future professional development sessions relate to literacy instruction?

Looking Ahead

Coaches are situated to see the active ingredients of literacy instruction on a daily basis as well as to promote these ingredients on a regular basis. This positions coaches to offer contextualized professional development opportunities that generate new understandings for faculty by sharing and analyzing examples of situated practice.

© 2017 by Rachael Gabriel and Sarah Woulfin, from *Making Teaching Evaluation Work*. Portsmouth, NH: Heinemann.

Pocket Version of the "Look-Fors" for Key Ingredients of Effective Literacy Instruction

Active Ingredients	In Observation . . .

Reading Accurately with a Purpose	1. You should be able to identify clear purposes for reading by doing the following:
	  a. Examine the board or recent posters and anchor charts to see if there is a visual reminder of a goal or reason for reading.
	  b. Ask students, "Why are you reading what you're reading?" or "What made you choose this text?"
	  c. Ask students what they will do as a result of their reading when they have finished it: "What will you be able to do/say/have when you have read this text?"
	2. Find evidence that students had the opportunity to read accurately by doing the following:
	  a. Notice whether more than one text was available for students to read during some part of the lesson either because students were given several options, a set of texts, or a choice of what to read.
	  b. Notice if students have opportunities to engage with the same text in more and less supported environments (whole group, small group, independently).
	  c. Notice if students had the opportunity to read and reread a text that was read aloud if it was particularly challenging: repeated reading of a challenging text, when supported by a model, indicates an investment in developing accuracy despite text complexity.

Writing with a Purpose and Audience	1. Both teachers and students reference a specific person or group (audience) when making decisions about what to write and how to represent ideas using words, sentences, and punctuation. Students should be able to fill in this blank: I/we are writing to ____ because/in order to _____. 2. The format of the writing task matches the stated purpose and audience every time, whether students are writing to demonstrate what they know about content, or writing in the context of a lesson focused on the writing process. 3. There is a balance between language and literature objectives within and across lessons to be sure students have both the *what* and the *why* of composition. If you see teachers addressing only one or the other, you might ask about when this will be balanced out in upcoming lessons.

Talking About Text with Teachers and Peers	1. Students have the opportunity to engage in back-and-forth discussions with the teacher (in a conference) or with peers (in small- or whole-group settings) that focus on something they wrote or read. 2. When students are talking in class, they are talking about texts they are preparing to read/write or in the process of reading/writing. 3. Teachers and students can name examples of discussions they have had, either individually or in groups, about the texts they are reading or writing this week. Evaluators that see reading/writing in progress might ask, "Have you gotten to talk to someone about this piece yet? Do you think you will?"
Discussing Models of Fluent Reading and Expert Writing	1. Teachers name and narrate what they are doing and why as they engage in reading or writing in front of students (model). They may leave a visual reminder of the processes they demonstrate, as steps, directions, reminders, or anchor charts to which students may refer. However, these charts cannot exist in isolation: their contents also require live demonstration and opportunities for student practice. 2. Descriptions of all steps of the writing process and exemplars of informal writing are outlined on anchor charts or other visual reminders. These are then demonstrated by teachers and practiced by students. 3. Students can describe or reference lists of criteria for success as readers and writers (e.g., what expert readers do, what expert writers do, what "we" are working toward).
Interventions That Support Individuals and Focus on Meaning	1. Students are grouped according to specific individual needs. 2. Students receive frequent, explicit coaching and feedback from someone who can identify difficulty and address it specifically. 3. Students regularly apply their skills to texts that carry meaning, which are selected by the teacher or student to ensure a good match for optimal practice. 4. Students are invited to discuss what they are doing, why, and how so that they not only perform but internalize the skills and strategies they will need for independent success.

Accountability First and Just Read Case Study

Though many instructional approaches align under one of these two contrasting philosophies, common examples might be Accountability First and Teachers' College Reading and Writing Project. Accountability First was a federally mandated, scripted program that was implemented by training the trainer at the state level, who then trained district leaders and school leaders so that information eventually trickled down to teachers. The focus of the program was on using a prescribed set of instructional materials and practices to generate data about student progress that could be used to hold teachers, coaches, and schools accountable for growth. This emphasis on compliance with prescribed instructional methods and assessments of reading skills for accountability purposes is a clear example of the Accountability First philosophy in action.

By contrast, Teachers College Reading and Writing Project is an example of the Just Read philosophy. The project advocates an approach, not a program, and is implemented by training teachers or teacher leaders individually to respond to students (information about instruction flows from the child up, rather than from the state down). Training for coaches was a later addition to the program's offerings, and training aimed at district- or state-level administrators doesn't exist. The focus of the program is on individual teachers identifying and addressing individual students' needs by watching their reading/writing in action during one-to-one conferences and delivering unscripted, individualized instruction at the point of need. This emphasis on the processes, rather than the outcomes, of reading and writing is a clear example of the Just Read philosophy in action.

To examine which philosophy (or combination) underlies instructional efforts in your building, list some of the features of your current approach and then sort them into the columns below. Though there are likely to be some practices in each column, where are the majority? Where would you like them to be for this year in your setting?

Accountability First	Just Read
• Develop proficient readers to raise test scores	• Develop students' love of books and reading
• Systemic reforms to raise achievement (state-down)	• Work with one child at a time to promote his or her development as a reader (child-up)
• Reliance on standards-aligned curriculum	• Reliance on authentic literature

Reflection Questions

- How do school and district leaders pressure you to teach reading?

- To what degree is your instruction controlled by standards, textbooks, and pacing guides?

- To what extent is your instruction individualized to match students' needs?

- What types of instructional materials do you rely on?

- What types of texts do students read in your classroom? Why?

- How do you assess students' growth as readers?

Create Your Own Case Study

Are your current practices more focused on accountability or support?

To begin a case study of your own literacy practices, jot down practices that match support and accountability. You could share this chart with a colleague or coach. You could also complete the chart as a team of educators or even across an entire school.

Areas	Current Practices (What does literacy instruction look like, sound like, feel like?)
Time use for reading • How is time balanced between teacher-directed instruction and independent reading? • Who controls teachers' use of instructional time?	
Setting a purpose for reading • How does the teacher introduce the goal of reading? • How does the teacher ask students to set a purpose for daily reading?	
Practicing accurate reading • What are students' opportunities to build fluency? • What types of texts are available for students to practice reading?	
Motivation to read • What strategies are used to motivate students as readers?	
Writing with purpose and audience • How does instruction balance standards-based writing instruction with student-directed writing? • Who controls/structures teachers' writing instruction?	
Talking about text • When and how do students have opportunities to talk about text? • How does the teacher facilitate conversations on text? • To what degree do students have ownership over the discussion of text?	

Areas	Current Practices (What does literacy instruction look like, sound like, feel like?)
Planning for intervention • When and how do teachers talk about individual students' progress? • How do assessment(s) and teacher input influence intervention placement? • To what extent are intervention activities individualized for students? • To what extent are intervention activities focused on meaning and connected to classwork?	

For Reflection
• What patterns do you notice across your instructional practices?   • Which areas do you feel more/less confident about?   • Are there areas that you'd like to shift practices toward support or accountability?

Surface Features and Underlying Processes

The table below shows some observable surface features alongside the processes and principles for instruction that they may represent. In the blanks below, work together with teachers, coaches, and administrators to match surface features to underlying processes to see how teacher knowledge translates into action and/or show the thinking behind the scenes.

Surface Features (Observable in a single lesson)	Underlying Processes (Uncover in discussion)
Short minilesson	Apprentice students into practices that support authentic reading and writing.
Long independent practice	
Conferencing	Demonstrate, name, practice, and give feedback on practices.
Modeled reading/writing	
Sharing/publication	Focus on the processes that allow meaning making and message sending.
Anchor charts	
Mentor texts	Teachers and texts are mentors, that is, examples to follow.
Classroom libraries	Practice is optimized for individuals by using choice and setting clear purposes.
Check the presence of these features to measure and sort.	*Analyze the uses of these principles to support and develop.*

Surface Features (Observable in a single lesson)	Underlying Processes (Uncover in discussion)
Check the presence of these features to measure and sort.	*Analyze the uses of these principles to support and develop.*

APPENDIX 6A

Structures for Framing Feedback as Learning Fuel

Data	Interpretation	Data with Interpretation
Everyone listened to directions.	That was a great lesson!	I thought it was great that everyone listened to directions.

1. Honestly Sandwich *What is good about this lesson or what good intention can you detect?*	"I see that you are keeping students' moods in mind when planning for the day before a vacation."
2. Specific *What data are you using? What is your interpretation of that data?*	"It looks like there is room for students to engage in reading/writing, but no structure for it during the movie."
3. Future Orientation *Based on this feedback, what should come next?*	"Before the next vacation, I wonder if you would try stopping the video once or twice for discussion and response so that fewer students sleep and more practice discussion/writing."

Questions to Ask When You Receive Poor Feedback

If the feedback is unclear:

1. Ask where the feedback is coming from and where it is going: "Tell me about why you think so? What do you think is a good next step?"
2. Clarify the advice: "So does this mean I should stop doing Daily Oral Language altogether, or just do it fewer times per week?"

If you disagree with the feedback:

1. What is right about the feedback and what do I disagree with?
2. What is different about the data or interpretation I have and those of the giver?
3. Have I ever heard feedback like this before? Why has it come up again?

Goal Envisioning Worksheet

This template is meant to illustrate what addressing a given goal would mean on a daily, weekly, monthly basis. As you are filling it out, ask yourself/team:

1. If we finalize this goal, what will I be doing on a monthly, weekly, and daily basis to meet it?
2. Is that the right work for me to be doing?
3. Are these daily, weekly, and monthly tasks important for student learning?
4. What might we cut or limit to make room for these tasks?

Goals	Approximate Time Needed
On a daily basis, I will	
On a weekly basis, I will	
On a monthly basis, I will	
I will know I have met the goal when	

Rubric for Identifying High-Quality Professional Development

Teachers, coaches, and administrators can use this tool, as individuals or in groups, to gauge—and reflect upon—the quality of professional development. While planning professional development (PD), you can refer to this rubric to intentionally incorporate high-quality features. After participating in or facilitating PD, you can use the rubric to capture reflections on the nature of the learning opportunities. Finally, you could complete the tool at the end of a semester or year to record impressions across multiple PDs. We include references for the evidence-based components of high-quality PD.

Domain	Below Standard	Meets Standard	Exemplary
Alignment	The content of the PD does not match existing needs at the teacher, school, and district levels.	The content of the PD relates to some growth areas for the teacher, school, or district.	The content of the PD is driven by needs at the district, school, and teacher levels and is tailored to particular experiences.
Content Focus	The PD is only weakly tied to core content and teaching strategies for that content.	The PD is related to core content but may not specifically address teaching strategies.	The PD addresses core content and presents multiple strategies for teaching that content.
Active Learning	The PD relies mainly on didactic presentation strategies.	The PD uses a range of presentation methods so that educators participate and engage during the training.	The PD centers upon practice-based opportunities to learn through doing.
Collaborative Learning Opportunities	Collaboration with other educators in the PD is incidental in nature.	Some collaboration with other educators over the course of the PD.	Extensive, purposeful collaboration and networking with other educators to cultivate strong, positive working relationships.
Follow-up	PD does not involve any follow-up or feedback.	There is some follow-up to the PD.	The PD incorporates and includes follow-up for participants to permit intensive contact with ideas and practices and ample time for ongoing learning and feedback.

© 2017 by Rachael Gabriel and Sarah Woulfin, from *Making Teaching Evaluation Work*. Portsmouth, NH: Heinemann.

References

http://www.gtlcenter.org/sites/default/files/docs/HighQualityProfessionalDevelopment.pdf.

http://www.sheeo.org/sites/default/files/PD%20Research%20-%20High%20Quality%20PD%20for%20 Teachers%2007-2013.pdf.

http://ies.ed.gov/ncee/edlabs/regions/southwest/pdf/rel_2007033.pdf.

https://learningforward.org/docs/pdf/nsdcstudy2009.pdf.

http://researchcollaboration.org/uploads/HQPD%20Generic%20Observation%20Checklist%20with%20 Examples%202016-01-22.PDF.

REFERENCES

Afflerbach, P. 2015. "How the Tests Used in Evaluating Reading Misrepresent Student Development and Teacher Effectiveness." In *Evaluating Literacy Instruction: Principles and Promising Practices*, edited by R. Gabriel and R. Allington. New York: Routledge.

Alexander, K. L., D. R. Entwisle, and L. S. Olson. 2007. "Lasting Consequences of the Summer Learning Gap." *American Sociological Review* 72 (2): 167–80. doi:10.1177/000312240707200202.

Allington, R. L. 1977. "If They Don't Read Much, How They Ever Gonna Get Good?" *Journal of Reading* 21: 57–61.

———. 2014. *What Really Matters in Response to Intervention*. New York: Pearson.

Allington, R., and P. Johnston. 2002. *Reading to Learn: Lessons from Exemplary Fourth-Grade Classrooms*. New York: Guilford Press.

Allington, R. L., K. McCuiston, and M. Billen. 2015. "What Research Says About Text Complexity and Learning to Read." *Reading Teacher* 68 (7): 491–501. doi:10.1002/trtr.1280.

Amrein-Beardsley, A. 2014. *Rethinking Value-Added Models in Education: Critical Perspectives on Tests and Assessment-Based Accountability*. New York: Routledge.

Amrein-Beardsley, A., J. Holloway-Libell, A. Cirell, A. Hays, and K. Chapman. 2015. "'Rational' Observational Systems of Educational Accountability and Reform." *Practical Assessment, Research and Evaluation* 20 (17). http://pareonline.net/getvn.asp?v=20&n=17.

Anderson, L. M., C. M. Evertson, and J. E. Brophy. 1979. "An Experimental Study of Effective Teaching in First-Grade Reading Groups." *The Elementary School Journal* 79 (4): 193–223.

Applebee, A. N., and J. A. Langer. 2009. "*EJ* Extra: What Is Happening to the Teaching of Writing?" *English Journal* 98 (5): 18–28.

———. 2011. "A Snapshot of Writing Instruction in Middle Schools and High Schools." *English Journal* 100 (6): 14–27.

Ball, D., and D. Cohen. 1999. "Developing Practice, Developing Practitioners." In *Teaching as the Learning Profession: Handbook for Policy and Practice*, edited by L. Darling-Hammond and G. Sykes, 3–32. San Francisco: Jossey-Bass.

Bryk, A. S., L. Gomez, A. Grunow, and P. LeMahieu. 2015. *Learning to Improve: How America's Schools Can Get Better at Getting Better*. Cambridge, MA: Harvard Educational Press.

Carnegie Council on Advancing Adolescent Literacy. 2010. *Time to Act: An Agenda for Advancing Adolescent Literacy for College and Career Success.* New York: Carnegie Corporation of New York.

Coburn, C. E. 2006. "Framing the Problem of Reading Instruction: Using Frame Analysis to Uncover the Microprocesses of Policy Implementation." *American Educational Research Journal* 43 (3): 343–79.

Connor, C. M., F. J. Morrison, B. J. Fishman, C. C. Ponitz, S. Glasney, P. S. Underwood, and C. Schatschneider. 2009. "The ISI Classroom Observation System: Examining the Literacy Instruction Provided to Individual Students." *Educational Researcher* 38 (2): 85–99.

Croninger, R., and L. Valli. 2009. "'Where Is the Action?' Challenges to Studying the Teaching of Reading in Elementary Classrooms." *Educational Researcher* 38 (2): 100–108.

Cunningham, A. E., and K. E. Stanovich. 1997. "Early Reading Acquisition and Its Relation to Reading Experience and Ability 10 Years Later." *Developmental Psychology* 33 (6): 934–45.

Darling-Hammond, L. 2010. "Steady Work: Finland Builds a Strong Teaching and Learning System." *Rethinking Schools* 24: 30–35. http://eric.ed.gov/?id=EJ932767.

Dennis, D. 2012. "Heterogeneity or Homogeneity: What Assessment Data Reveal About Struggling Readers." *Journal of Literacy Research* 45 (1): 3–21.

Donaldson, M., C. Cobb, K. LeChasseur, R. Gabriel, R. Gonzalez, S. Woulfin, and A. Makuch. 2013. "An Evaluation of the Pilot Implementation of Connecticut's System for Educator Evaluation and Development." Interim Report. UConn Center for Education Policy Analysis. Storrs, CT: University of Connecticut.

DuFour, R. 2003. "Ask for More but Focus on Doing Better with What's at Hand." *Journal of Staff Development* 24 (3): 67–68.

Duke, N. K. 2000. "For the Rich It's Richer: Print Experiences and Environments Offered to Children in Very Low- and Very High-Socioeconomic Status First-Grade Classrooms." *American Educational Research Journal* 37 (2): 441–78. doi:10.3102/00028312037002441.

Echevarria, J., M. E. Vogt, and D. Short. 2007. *Making Content Comprehensible for English Learners: The SIOP Model.* 3rd ed. Boston: Pearson Allyn & Bacon.

Ehri, L. C., L. G. Dreyer, B. Flugman, and A. Gross. 2007. "Reading Rescue: An Effective Tutoring Intervention Model for Language Minority Students Who Are Struggling Readers in First Grade." *American Educational Research Journal* 44 (2): 414–48.

Emery, T. 2007. "In Tennessee, goats eat the 'vine that ate the south'." *New York Times*, June 5, A16. Retrieved from: http://www.nytimes .com/2007/06/05/us/05goats.html.

Fitzgerald, J. 2001. "Can Minimally Trained College Student Volunteers Help Young At-Risk Children to Read Better?" *Reading Research Quarterly* 36 (1): 28–46. http://www.jstor.org/stable/748126.

Fulmer, S. M., S. K. D'Mello, A. Strain, and A. C. Graesser. 2015. "Interest-Based Text Preference Moderates the Effect of Text Difficulty on Engagement and Learning." *Contemporary Educational Psychology* 41: 98–110.

Gabriel, R. In press. "Rubrics and Reflection: A Discursive Analysis of Observation Debrief Conversations Between Novice Teach for America Teachers and Mentors." *Action in Teacher Education.*

Gabriel, R. 2015. "Not Whether, but How: Asking the Right Questions in Teacher Performance Assessment." *Language Arts* 93 (2): 120–27.

Gabriel, R., R. Allington, and M. Billen. 2012a. "Background Knowledge and the Magazine Reading They Choose." *Voices from the Middle* 20 (1): 52–58.

———. 2012b. "Middle Schoolers and Magazines: What Teachers Can Learn from Students' Leisure Reading Habits." *The Clearing House* 85 (5): 186–91.

Gabriel, R., and H. Dostal. 2015a. "Interactive Writing in the Disciplines: A Common Core Approach to Writing Instruction Across Content Areas." *The Clearing House* 88 (2): 66–71.

Gabriel, R., and H. Dostal. 2015b. *Language Diversity, Literacy Difficulties, and Imagining for Equity*. Carlsbad, CA: Literacy Research Association.

Gabriel, R., and J. N. Lester. 2013a. "The Romance Quest of Education Reform: A Discourse Analysis of the *LA Times*' Reports on Value-Added Measurement Teacher Effectiveness." *Teacher's College Record* 115 (12): 1–32.

Gabriel, R., and J. N. Lester. 2013b. "Sentinels Guarding the Grail: Value-Added Measurement and the Quest for Education Reform." *Educational Policy Analysis Archives* 20 (9). http://epaa.asu.edu/ojs/article/view/1165.

Gabriel, R., and E. Rojas. 2015. "Five Questions Teachers of Culturally, Linguistically, and Socially Diverse Students Want to Be Asked in Their Teacher Evaluations." *Principal Leadership* 15 (6): 28–32.

Gabriel, R., C. Wenz, and H. Dostal. 2016. "Disciplinary Text-Dependent Questions: Questioning for Learning in the Disciplines." *The Clearing House* 89 (6): 202–207. doi:10.1080/00098655.2016.1209154.

Gage, N. L., and M. C. Needles. 1989. "Process-Product Research on Teaching." *Elementary School Journal* 89: 253–300.

Gambrell, L. B. 1996. "Creating Classroom Cultures That Foster Motivation to Read." *Reading Teacher* 50 (1): 4–25.

Garan, E. 2002. *In Defense of Our Children: When Politics, Profits, and Education Collide*. Portsmouth, NH: Heinemann.

———. 2004. *Resisting Reading Mandates: How to Triumph with the Truth*. Portsmouth, NH: Heinemann.

Gawande, A. 2010. *The Checklist Manifesto: How to Get Things Right*. New York: Metropolitan Books.

Gee, J. P. 2001. "Identity as an Analytic Lens for Research in Education." *Review of Research in Education* 25 (1): 99–125.

Georgetown College. 2016. *CRIOP: Seven CRIOP Elements*. Retrieved from http://www.georgetowncollege.edu/ccrp/seven-criop-elements/.

Glaser, J., and R. Glaser. 2014. "The Neurochemistry of Positive Conversations." *Harvard Business Review* (June). https://hbr.org/2014/06/the-neurochemistry-of-positive-conversations.

Goodwin, B., and K. Miller. 2012. "Good Feedback Is Targeted, Specific, Timely." *Educational Leadership* 70 (1): 82–83.

Graham, S., and K. Harris. 2016. "A Path to Better Writing: Evidence-Based Practices in the Classroom." *The Reading Teacher* 69 (4): 359–65.

Graham, S., A. Capizzi, K. R. Harris, M. Hebert, and P. Morphy. 2014. "Teaching Writing to Middle School Students: A National Survey." *Reading & Writing* 27 (6): 1015–42. doi:10.1007/s11145-013-9495-7.

Graham, S., and M. Hebert. 2010. *Writing to Read: Evidence for How Writing Can Improve Reading*. New York: Carnegie Corporation.

Graham, S., and D. Perin. 2007. *Writing Next: Effective Strategies to Improve Writing of Adolescents in Middle and High Schools*. New York: Carnegie Corporation.

Grossman, P., S. Loeb, J. Cohen, and J. Wyckoff. 2013. "Measure for Measure: The Relationship Between Measures of Instructional Practice in Middle School English Language Arts and Teachers' Value-Added." *American Journal of Education* 119 (3): 445–70.

Guthrie, J. T., and A. Wigfield. 2000. "Engagement and Motivation in Reading." In *Handbook of Reading Research: Volume III*, edited by M. L. Kamil, P. B. Mosenthal, P. D. Pearson, and R. Barr, 403–22. Mahwah, NJ: Lawrence Erlbaum Associates.

Guthrie, J., A. Wigfield, J. Metsala, and K. Cox. 1999. "Motivational and Cognitive Predictors of Text Comprehension and Reading Amount." *Scientific Studies of Reading* 3 (3): 231–56.

Hall, G. E., D. J. Dirksen, and A. A. George. 2008. *Measuring Implementation in Schools: Levels of Use*. Austin, TX: Southwest Educational Development Laboratory.

Hattie, J. A. C. 2009. *Visible Learning: A Synthesis of Over 800 Meta-Analyses Relating to Achievement*. London, UK: Routledge.

Heritage, M. 2010. *Formative Assessment: Making It Happen in the Classroom*. Thousands Oaks, CA: Corwin Press.

Hiebert, E. H. 2005. "The Effects of Text Difficulty on Second Graders' Fluency Development." *Reading Psychology* 26 (2): 183–209. doi:10.1080/02702710590930528t.

Hiebert, E. H., S. W. Valencia, and P. P. Afflerbach. 1994. "Understand Authentic Reading Assessment: Definitions and Perspectives." In *Authentic Reading Assessment: Practices and Possibilities*, edited by S. W. Valencia, E. H. Hiebert, and P. P. Afflerbach, 6–21. Newark, DE: International Reading Association.

Hill, H., and P. Grossman. 2016. "Learning from Teacher Observations: Challenges and Opportunities Posed by New Teacher Evaluation Systems." Working Paper. Cambridge, MA: Harvard School of Education.

Hong, G., and Y. Hong. 2009. "Reading Instruction Time and Homogenous Grouping in Kindergarten: An Application of Marginal Mean Weighting Through Stratification." *Educational Evaluation and Policy Analysis* 31 (1): 54–81.

Johnston, P. 2005. "Literacy Assessment and the Future." *The Reading Teacher* 58: 684–86. doi:10.1598/RT.58.7.9.

Kane, T. 2015. "Gathering Feedback for Teaching." Gates Foundation. http://k12education.gatesfoundation.org/wp-content/uploads/2016/06/MET_Gathering_Feedback_for_Teaching_Summary1.pdf.

Klauda, S. L., and J. T. Guthrie. 2015. "Comparing Relations of Motivation, Engagement, and Achievement Among Struggling and Advanced Adolescent Readers." *Reading and Writing* 28 (2): 239–69.

Kraft, M. A., and A. F. Gilmour. 2016. "Revisiting the Widget Effect: Teacher Evaluation Reforms and the Distribution of Teacher Effectiveness." Working Paper. Providence, RI: Brown University.

Lavigne, A., and T. Oberg de la Gaza. 2015. "The Practice and Evaluation of Culturally Responsive Literacy for English Language Learners in the 21st Century." In *Evaluating Literacy Instruction: Principles and Promising Practices*, edited by R. Gabriel and R. Allington. New York: Routledge.

Leach, J. M., H. S. Scarborough, and L. Rescorla. 2003. "Late-Emerging Reading Disabilities." *Journal of Educational Psychology* 95 (2): 211–24.

Lee, C. D., and A. Spratley. 2010. "Reading in the Disciplines: The Challenges of Adolescent Literacy." New York: Carnegie Corporation of New York.

Lesaux, N. K., and M. J. Kieffer. 2010. "Exploring Sources of Reading Comprehension Difficulties Among Language Minority Learners and Their Classmates in Early Adolescence." *American Educational Research Journal* 47 (3): 596–632.

Lopez, F. 2011. "The Nongeneralizability of Classroom Dynamics as Predictors of Achievement for Hispanic Students in Upper Elementary Grades." *Hispanic Journal of Behavioral Sciences* 33 (3): 350–76.

Lortie, D. 1975. *Schoolteacher: A Sociological Study.* Chicago: University of Chicago Press.

McGonigal, K. 2015. *The Upside of Stress: Why Stress Is Good for You and How to Get Good at It.* New York: Avery.

McLaughlin, B., and J. Smink. 2009. Summer Learning: Moving from the Periphery to the Core. *The Progress of Education Reform* 10 (3). Denver, CO: Education Commission of the States. www.ecs.org/clearinghouse/80/99/8099.pdf.

McQuillan, J., and J. Au. 2001. "The Effect of Print Access on Reading Frequency." *Reading Psychology* 22 (3): 225–48.

MET Project. 2012. *Gathering Feedback for Teaching Combining High-Quality Observations with Student Surveys and Achievement Gains.* files.eric.ed.gov/fulltext/ED540960.pdf.

Metcalfe, J., N. Kornell, and B. Finn. 2009. "Delayed Versus Immediate Feedback in Children's and Adults' Vocabulary Learning." *Memory and Cognition* 37 (8): 1077–87.

Morgan, A., B. R. Wilcox, and J. L. Eldredge. 2000. "Effect of Difficulty Levels on Second-Grade Delayed Readers Using Dyad Reading." *The Journal of Educational Research* 94 (2): 113–19.

Mory, E. 2004. "Feedback Research Revisited." In *Handbook of Research on Educational Communications and Technology*, 2nd ed., edited by D. Jonassen, 745–83. Mahwah, NJ: Lawrence Erlbaum.

National Reading Panel (U.S.), and National Institute of Child Health and Human Development (U.S.). 2000. *Report of the National Reading Panel: Teaching Children to Read: An Evidence-Based Assessment of the Scientific Research Literature on Reading and Its Implications for Reading Instruction: Reports of the Subgroups.* Washington, DC: National Institute of Child Health and Human Development, National Institutes of Health.

Neuman, S. B. 1999. "Books Make a Difference: A Study of Access to Literacy." *Reading Research Quarterly* 34 (3): 2–31.

Nystrand, M. 2006. "Research on the Role of Classroom Discourse as It Affects Reading Comprehension." *Research in the Teaching of English* 40: 392–412.

O'Connor, R. E., K. M. Bell, K. R. Harty, L. K. Larkin, S. M. Sackor, and N. Zigmond. 2002. "Teaching Reading to Poor Readers in the Intermediate Grades: A Comparison of Text Difficulty." *Journal of Educational Psychology* 94 (3): 474–85.

Papay, J. 2011. "Different Tests, Different Answers: The Stability of Teacher Value-Added Estimates Across Outcome Measures." *American Educational Research Journal* 48 (1): 463–93.

Park, V., A. J. Daly, and A. W. Guerra. 2013. "Strategic Framing: How Leaders Craft the Meaning of Data Use for Equity and Learning." *Educational Policy* 27 (4): 645–75. doi:10.1177/0895904811429295.

Pianta, R. C., K. M. La Paro, and B. K. Hamre. 2008. *Classroom Assessment Scoring System: Manual K–3*. Baltimore, MD: Paul H. Brookes.

Polikoff, M. S., and A. C. Porter. 2014. "Instructional Alignment as a Measure of Teaching Quality." *Educational Evaluation and Policy Analysis* 36 (4): 399–416. doi:10.3102/0162373714531851.

Powell, R., and E. C. Rightmeyer, eds. 2011. *Literacy for All Students: An Instructional Framework for Closing the Gap*. New York: Routledge.

Raphael, T. E., K. H. Au, and S. R. Goldman. 2009. "Whole School Instructional Improvement Through the Standards-Based Change Process." In *Changing Literacies for Changing Times: An Historical Perspective on Reading Research, Public Policy, and Classroom Practices*, edited by James V. Hoffman and Yetta Goodman, 198–229. New York: Routledge.

Rupp, A. A., and N. K. Lesaux. 2006. "Meeting Expectations? An Empirical Investigation of a Standards-Based Assessment of Reading Comprehension." *Educational Evaluation and Policy Analysis* 28 (4): 315–33.

Southwest Educational Development Laboratory (SEDL). 2016. "Concerns-Based Adoption Model." www.sedl.org/cbam/.

Spear-Swerling, L. 2014. *The Power of RTI and Reading Profiles: A Blueprint for Solving Reading Problems*. Baltimore: Brookes.

Stahl, S. A., and K. Heubach. 2005. "Fluency-Oriented Reading Instruction." *Journal of Literacy Research* 37: 25–60.

Stanovich, K. E. 1986. "Matthew Effects in Reading: Some Consequences of Individual Differences in the Acquisition of Literacy." *Reading Research Quarterly* 21 (4): 360–407.

Stanulis, R. N., K. S. Cooper, B. Dear, A. M. Johnston, and R. R. Richard-Todd. 2016. "Teacher-Led Reforms Have a Big Advantage—Teachers." *Phi Delta Kappan* 97 (7): 53–57. doi:10.1177/0031721716641650.

Steinberg, M., and L. Sartain. 2015. "Does Better Observation Make Better Teachers?" *Education Next*. http://educationnext.org/better-observation-make-better-teachers/.

Stone, D., and S. Heen. 2015. *Thanks for the Feedback: The Science and Art of Receiving Feedback Well*. New York: Viking Press.

Summitt, P., and S. Jenkins. 2014. *Sum It Up: A Thousand and Ninety-Eight Victories, a Couple of Irrelevant Losses, and a Life in Perspective*. New York: Three Rivers Press.

Taylor, B. M., P. D. Pearson, K. F. Clark, and S. Walpole. 1999. "Effective Schools/Accomplished Teachers." *The Reading Teacher* 53: 156–59.

U.S. Department of Education. 2008. *Reading First Impact Study: Final Report*. NCEE 2009 4038. Retrieved from https://ies.ed.gov/ncee/pubs/20094038/summ_b.asp.

U.S. Department of Education, Institute of Education Sciences, National Center for Education Statistics, National Assessment of Educational Progress (NAEP). 2015. Reading Assessment. http://www.nationsreportcard.gov/reading_math_2015/#?grade=4.

U.S. National Commission on Excellence in Education. 1983. *A Nation at Risk: The Imperative for Educational Reform: A Report to the Nation and the Secretary of Education, United States Department of Education*. Washington, DC: U.S. National Commission on Excellence in Education.

Valencia, S. 2010. "Reader Profiles and Reading Disabilities." In *Handbook of Reading Disabilities Research*, edited by R. Allington and A. McGill-Franzen, 25–35. Mahwah, NJ: Lawrence Erlbaum.

Valencia, S., and M. Riddle Buly. 2004. "Behind Test Scores: What Struggling Readers Really Need." *The Reading Teacher* 57 (6): 520–31.

Valencia, S. W., E. H. Hiebert, and P. P. Afflerbach. 2004. *Authentic Reading Assessment: Practices and Possibilities*. Newark, DE: International Reading Association.

Valencia, S. W., N. A. Place, S. D. Martin, and P. L. Grossman. 2006. "Curriculum Materials for Elementary Reading: Shackles and Scaffolds for Four Beginning Teachers Author(s)." *The Elementary School Journal* 107 (1): 93–120. doi:10.1086/509528.

Vygotsky, L. S. 1978. *Mind in Society: The Development of Higher Psychological Processes*. Cambridge, MA: Harvard University Press.

Weisberg, D., S. Sexton, J. Mulhern, and D. Keeling, for The New Teacher Project. 2009. "The Widget Effect: Our National Failure to Acknowledge and Act on Differences in Teacher Effectiveness." 2nd ed. Brooklyn, NY: The New Teacher Project. http://tntp.org/assets/documents/TheWidgetEffect_2nd_ed.pdf.

Whitehurst, G. J., M. M. Chingos, and K. M. Lindquist. 2015. "Getting Classroom Observations Right." *Education Next* 15 (1).

Wiliam, D. 2009. *Assessment for Learning: Why, What, and How?* London: Institute of Education Press, University of London.

Willingham, D. T. 2009. "Reading Is Not a Skill and Why This Is a Problem for the Draft National Standards." *Washington Post Answer Sheet.* http://voices.washingtonpost.com/answer-sheet/daniel-willingham /willingham-reading-is-not-a-sk.html.

Worthy, M. J., M. Moorman, and M. Turner. 1999. "What Johnny Likes to Read Is Hard to Find in School." *Reading Research Quarterly* 34 (1): 12–27.